Global Politics

ROBERT MURPHY WITH CHARLES GLEEK

SERIES EDITOR: CHRISTIAN BRYAN

for the IB Diploma

essentials

Published by Pearson Education Limited, Edinburgh Gate, Harlow, Essex, CM20 2JE.

www.pearsonglobalschools.com

Text © Pearson Education Limited 2016

Edited by Sarah Lustig
Proofread by Sze Kiu Yeung
Typeset by Ken Vail Graphic Design Limited

The rights of Robert Murphy and Charles Gleek to be identified as authors of this work has been asserted by them in accordance with the Copyright, Designs and Patents Act 1988.

First published 2016

ARP impression 98

British Library Cataloguing in Publication Data
A catalogue record for this book is available from the British Library

ISBN 9781447999263
eBook only ISBN 9781447999270

Printed and bound in Great Britain by Ashford Colour Press Ltd.

Acknowledgements

The authors and publisher would like to thank:
Oscar Van Nooijen for his inspiration and expert help in planning and reviewing.
Sylvi Wirtjes for her contribution and input to the project's early stages.
Christian Bryan for his help in writing the Development unit.
Laurence Ward for his early review and his input to the Global challenge presentation material.
Jo Kent for her EAL review.
Gary Goodwin for creating the cartoon that appears on page 1.

The author and publisher would like to thank the following individuals and organisations for permission to reproduce copyright material:

Figures
Figures 1.2, 1.3 from *The Economist Pocket World in Figures*, 2016 Edition, Economist Books, London (2015); Figure 3.4 from *Green Economics*, London: Earthscan (Scott Cato, M. 2009) Fig. 3.1, pp.36-37.

Tables
Table on page 5 from *The Economist Pocket World in Figures*, 2016 Edition, Economist Books, London (2015).

Every effort has been made to contact copyright holders of material reproduced in this book. Any omissions will be rectified in subsequent printings if notice is given to the publishers.

Text extracts relating to the IB syllabus and assessment have been reproduced from IBO documents. Our thanks go to the International Baccalaureate for permission to reproduce its intellectual copyright. This material has been developed independently by the publisher and the content is in no way connected with or endorsed by the International Baccalaureate (IB). International Baccalaureate ® is a registered trademark of the International Baccalaureate Organization.

Websites

Pearson Education Limited is not responsible for the content of any external internet sites. It is essential for tutors to preview each website before using it in class so as to ensure that the URL is still accurate, relevant and appropriate. We suggest that tutors bookmark useful websites and consider enabling students to access them through the school/college intranet.

Dedications

For my parents, Andrew and Monica.

And with special thanks to my students and colleagues at Wellington College, especially Anthony Seldon.

Contents

Welcome to your Essentials guide to Global Politics. This book has been designed to solve the key problems of many IB Diploma students. It will:

- relate material you have been taught to the syllabus goals and outcomes
- provide examples and case studies which build your understanding of the key concepts
- help you demonstrate your understanding of key concepts in an exam situation within a strict time limit.

Who should use Essentials guides?

Essentials guides serve as highly effective summaries and have been carefully designed with all IB students in mind.

However, the guides also deal with the particular interests of IB students whose first language is not English, and who would like further support. As a result, the content in all Essentials guides has been edited by an EAL (English as an additional language) expert to make sure that:

- the language used is clear and accessible
- key terms are explained
- essential vocabulary is defined and reinforced.

Key features of an Essentials guide

Reduced content: Essentials guides are not intended to be comprehensive textbooks – they contain the essential information you need to understand and respond to the key concepts in the IB Global Politics Guide. This allows you to understand material quickly and still be confident you are meeting the essential aims of the syllabus. We have reduced the number of words as much as possible to ensure everything you read has clear meaning. Each page is clearly related to the IB Global Politics Guide and will help you in the exam.

Format and approach: The content of the book is organized according to the units and concepts in the IB Global Politics Guide. Each concept is looked at separately so that you can study each one without having read or understood previous sections. This allows you to use the book as a first text, or a revision guide, or as a way to help you understand material you have been given from other sources.

Key ideas: Each sub-topic starts with a key idea, which gives a simple introduction to the topic and an idea of the main learning point.

Key idea:

Human rights are the indivisible rights which all human beings are entitled to by virtue of their humanity, without discrimination.

Articulation sentences: Articulation sentences are designed to summarize the main point within a piece of text to help you with understanding.

 Articulation sentences:

Positive human rights are those in which the government must take action to protect the people; negative rights require the government not to act to allow certain freedoms.

Vocabulary and synonym boxes: Useful words and phrases are colour-coded in the text and given matching colour-coded explanations in the margins. There are three different sets: vocabulary related to the topic, synonyms, and **general vocabulary**. These are included to help identify and support your understanding of academic and difficult words. In order to make the text more accessible to students whose first language is not English, we have maintained an academic tone but removed unnecessary vocabulary. However, at the same time we have ensured that the complexity of the content is at the level required by successful IB Diploma students.

Subject vocabulary

bilateral involving two groups or nations

Synonyms

pseudo .... having the appearance of, but not being, real

---

General vocabulary

oil fields areas where there is oil under the land or under the bottom of the sea

---

Other features of this guide

Challenge yourself boxes: These contain open questions that are linked to the IB's Approaches To Learning (ATL) and encourage you to think about the topic in more depth, or to make detailed connections with other topics. They are designed to make you think, work together and carry out additional research.

Global Politics is a new concept-based course and as such, the **Key concepts** should be constantly referred to throughout the four core units, the engagement activity and the HL extension. We include the 16 concepts on p.vi–vii and regularly refer to these definitions in order to provide the conceptual framework you need to access and understand the political issues examined.

CHALLENGE YOURSELF

Research and Thinking skills

Look up the Fairtrade Foundation. They aim to ensure workers receive fair pay. On their website you can read about the world sugar trade. Which countries are finding it difficult to trade sugar and why? Has globalization of the sugar trade benefited those countries?

We have also provided the **Command terms** on p.x so that you are thinking about these for the whole period you use this guide and not just at revision time.

Engagement activity, Exam support and Extended Essay sections: These are intended to help you design, research and write your own activities, responses and essays. They provide useful guidance and explain what is required to achieve the top marks.

eText and audio: In the accompanying eText you will find a complete digital version of the book. There are also links to spoken audio files of the vocabulary terms and definitions to help with comprehension and pronunciation. In addition, all the vocabulary lists are located together as downloadable files.

Above all, we hope this book helps you to understand and consolidate your Global Politics course more easily, helping you to achieve the highest possible result in your exams and internally-assessed activities.

Key concepts

The following 16 key concepts weave a conceptual thread through the course. They should be explored both when working with the four core units, the engagement activity and the HL extension, in order to equip students with a conceptual framework with which to access and understand the political issues examined.

Concept	Explanation
Power	Power is a central concept in the study of global politics and a key focus of the course. Power can be seen as ability to effect change and, rather than being viewed as a unitary or independent force, is as an aspect of relations among people functioning within a social organization. Contested relationships between people and groups of people dominate politics, particularly in this era of increased globalization, and so understanding the dynamics of power plays a prominent role in understanding global politics.
Sovereignty	Sovereignty characterizes a state's independence, its control over territory and its ability to govern itself. How states use their sovereign power is at the heart of many important issues in global politics. Some theorists argue that sovereign power is increasingly being eroded by aspects of globalization such as global communication and trade, which states cannot always fully control. Others argue that sovereign states exercise a great deal of power when acting in their national interest and that this is unlikely to change.
Legitimacy	Legitimacy refers to an actor or an action being commonly considered acceptable and provides the fundamental basis or rationale for all forms of governance and other ways of exercising power over others. The most accepted contemporary source of legitimacy in a state is some form of democracy or constitutionalism whereby the governed have a defined and periodical opportunity to choose who they wish to exercise power over them. Other sources of legitimacy are suggested in states in which such an opportunity does not exist. Within any proposed overall framework of legitimacy, individual actions by a state can be considered more or less legitimate. Other actors of global politics and their actions can also be evaluated from the perspective of legitimacy.
Interdependence	In global politics, the concept of interdependence most often refers to the mutual reliance between and among groups, organizations, geographic areas and/or states for access to resources that sustain living arrangements. Often, this mutual reliance is economic (such as trade), but can also have a security dimension (such as defence arrangements) and, increasingly, a sustainability dimension (such as environmental treaties). Globalization has increased interdependence, while often changing the relationships of power among the various actors engaged in global politics.
Human rights	Human rights are basic claims and entitlements that, many argue, one should be able to exercise simply by virtue of being a human being. Many contemporary thinkers argue they are essential for living a life of dignity, are inalienable, and should be accepted as universal. The Universal Declaration of Human Rights adopted by the UN in 1948 is recognized as the beginning of the formal discussion of human rights around the world. Critics argue that human rights are a Western, or at least culturally relative, concept.
Justice	There are a number of different interpretations of the concept of justice. It is often closely associated with the idea of fairness and with individuals getting what they deserve, although what is meant by desert is also contested. One avenue is to approach justice through the idea of rights, and what individuals can legitimately expect of one another or of their government. Some theorists also argue that equality not only in the institutions and procedures of a society but also in capabilities or well-being outcomes is required for justice to be realized.
Liberty	The concept of liberty refers to having freedom and autonomy. It is often divided into positive and negative liberty, with *negative liberty* defined as individuals having the freedom from external coercion and *positive liberty* defined as individuals having the autonomy to carry out their own rational will. Some scholars reject this distinction and argue that in practice, one form of liberty cannot exist without the other. It is also questioned if such an understanding of liberty is sufficient for an interdependent world, in which the seeming freedom and autonomy of some may depend on lack of some forms of liberty for others. Hence, debates on equality inform our understanding of liberty as well.

Concept	Explanation
Equality	Egalitarian theories are based on a concept of equality that all people, or groups of people, are seen as having the same intrinsic value. Equality is therefore closely linked to justice and fairness, as egalitarians argue that justice can only exist if there is equality. Increasingly, with growing polarization within societies, equality is also linked to liberty, as different people have differing possibilities to be free and autonomous.
Development	Development is a sustained increase in the standard of living and well-being of a level of social organization. Many consider it to involve increased income; better access to basic goods and services; improvements in education, healthcare and public health; well-functioning institutions; decreased inequality; reduced poverty and unemployment; and more sustainable production and consumption patterns. The focus of development debates in contemporary global politics is on issues faced by developing countries, and on the imperative of shifting the focus from modernization (seen as Westernization). However, all societies and communities face questions about how to best promote well-being and reduce ill-being.
Globalization	Globalization is a process by which the world's local, national and regional economies, societies and cultures are becoming increasingly integrated and connected. The term refers to the reduction of barriers and borders, as people, goods, services and ideas flow more freely between different parts of the world. Globalization is a process that has been taking place for centuries but the pace has quickened in recent decades, facilitated by developments in transportation and communication technology, and powered by cheap energy. It is now widely acknowledged that globalization has both benefits and drawbacks and that its benefits are not evenly distributed.
Inequality	Inequality refers to a state of affairs where equality between people or groups of people is not realized and the consequent potential compromises of justice and liberty. Inequality often manifests itself through unequal access to resources that are needed to sustain life and develop individuals and communities. Consequently, the concept is closely connected to discussions of power and of who holds the rights to these resources and their proceeds. Inequality can be examined both as a phenomenon within and between societies.
Sustainability	Definitions of sustainability begin with the idea that development should meet the needs of the present without compromising the ability of future generations to meet their needs. Sustainability today has three fields of debate — environmental, sociopolitical and economic. In global politics, mechanisms and incentives required for political institutions, economic actors and individuals to take a longer term and more inclusive well-being perspective in their decision-making are particularly important.
Peace	Peace is often defined as both the absence of conflict and violence as well as a state of harmonious relations. Many also refer to peace as a personal state of non-conflict, particularly with oneself and with one's relationship to others. Peace is the ultimate goal of many organizations that monitor and regulate social relationships.
Conflict	Conflict is the dynamic process of actual or perceived opposition between individuals or groups. This could be opposition over positions, interests or values. Most theorists would distinguish between non-violent and violent conflict. In this distinction, non-violent conflict can be a useful mechanism for social change and transformation, while violent conflict is harmful and requires conflict resolution.
Violence	Violence is often defined as physical or psychological force afflicted upon another being. In the context of global politics, it could be seen as anything someone does that prevents others from reaching their full potential. This broader definition would encompass unequal distribution of power that excludes entire groups from accessing resources essential for improved living standards or well-being, and discriminatory practices that exclude entire groups of people from accessing certain resources.
Non-violence	Non-violence is the practice of advocating one's own or others' rights without physically harming the opponent. It often involves actively opposing the system that is deemed to be unjust, through for example boycotts, demonstrations and civil disobedience. Theorists argue that non-violence can often draw attention to a conflict situation and that it could provide a fertile basis for post-conflict transformation.

How to use your enhanced eBook

Jump to any page

Switch from single- to double-page view

Highlight parts of the text

Create notes

Search the whole book

Zoom

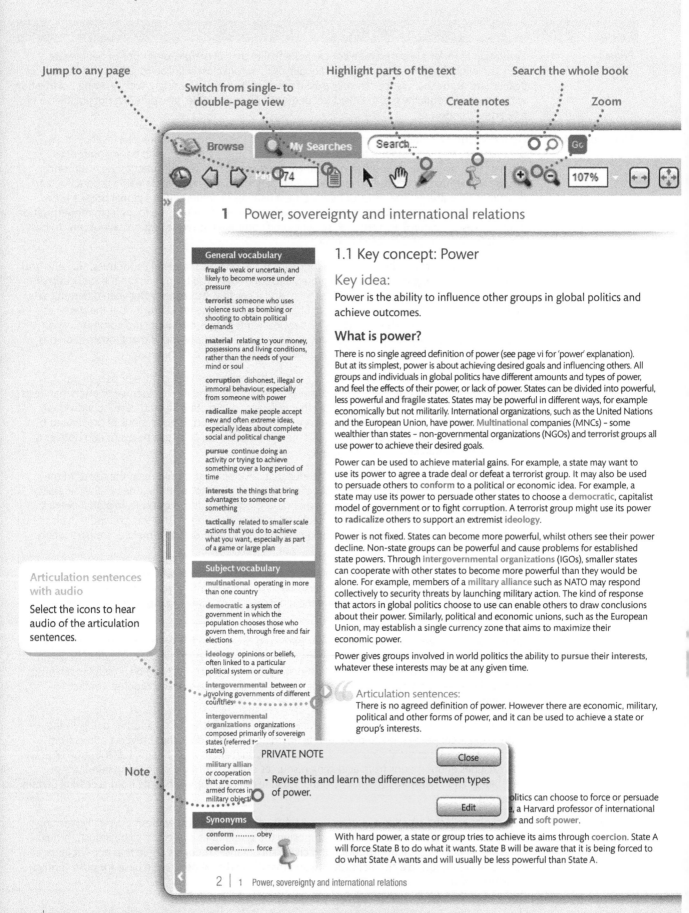

Articulation sentences with audio

Select the icons to hear audio of the articulation sentences.

Note

1 Power, sovereignty and international relations

General vocabulary

fragile weak or uncertain, and likely to become worse under pressure

terrorist someone who uses violence such as bombing or shooting to obtain political demands

material relating to your money, possessions and living conditions, rather than the needs of your mind or soul

corruption dishonest, illegal or immoral behaviour, especially from someone with power

radicalize make people accept new and often extreme ideas, especially ideas about complete social and political change

pursue continue doing an activity or trying to achieve something over a long period of time

interests the things that bring advantages to someone or something

tactically related to smaller scale actions that you do to achieve what you want, especially as part of a game or large plan

Subject vocabulary

multinational operating in more than one country

democratic a system of government in which the population chooses those who govern them, through free and fair elections

ideology opinions or beliefs, often linked to a particular political system or culture

intergovernmental between or involving governments of different countries

intergovernmental organizations organizations composed primarily of sovereign states (referred to as states)

military allian or cooperation that are commi armed forces in military objecti

Synonyms

conform .... obey

coercion .... force

1.1 Key concept: Power

Key idea:

Power is the ability to influence other groups in global politics and achieve outcomes.

What is power?

There is no single agreed definition of power (see page vi for 'power' explanation). But at its simplest, power is about achieving desired goals and influencing others. All groups and individuals in global politics have different amounts and types of power, and feel the effects of their power, or lack of power. States can be divided into powerful, less powerful and fragile states. States may be powerful in different ways, for example economically but not militarily. International organizations, such as the United Nations and the European Union, have power. Multinational companies (MNCs) – some wealthier than states – non-governmental organizations (NGOs) and terrorist groups all use power to achieve their desired goals.

Power can be used to achieve material gains. For example, a state may want to use its power to agree a trade deal or defeat a terrorist group. It may also be used to persuade others to conform to a political or economic idea. For example, a state may use its power to persuade other states to choose a democratic, capitalist model of government or to fight corruption. A terrorist group might use its power to radicalize others to support an extremist ideology.

Power is not fixed. States can become more powerful, whilst others see their power decline. Non-state groups can be powerful and cause problems for established state powers. Through intergovernmental organizations (IGOs), smaller states can cooperate with other states to become more powerful than they would be alone. For example, members of a military alliance such as NATO may respond collectively to security threats by launching military action. The kind of response that actors in global politics choose to use can enable others to draw conclusions about their power. Similarly, political and economic unions, such as the European Union, may establish a single currency zone that aims to maximize their economic power.

Power gives groups involved in world politics the ability to pursue their interests, whatever these interests may be at any given time.

> **Articulation sentences:**
> There is no agreed definition of power. However there are economic, military, political and other forms of power, and it can be used to achieve a state or group's interests.

PRIVATE NOTE [Close]

– Revise this and learn the differences between types of power.

[Edit]

...olitics can choose to force or persuade ..., a Harvard professor of international ...r and soft power.

With hard power, a state or group tries to achieve its aims through coercion. State A will force State B to do what it wants. State B will be aware that it is being forced to do what State A wants and will usually be less powerful than State A.

See the definitions of key terms in the glossary

Switch to whiteboard view

Create a bookmark

With soft power, a state or group tries to achieve its aims through persuasion or influence. State A will persuade State B to do what it wants, with or without State B being aware that this is what State A wants. Nye describes this as 'the power to get others to want what you want'. States and groups that use soft power can use culture, foreign policy (if ethical and exemplary) and political values (for example democracy, rule of law, tolerance, justice) to persuade other states (see page vi for 'justice' explanation). An unpopular or unethical foreign policy (such as the 2003 invasion of Iraq or the 2014 annexation of Crimea) or a lack of political freedom at home (such as in China) may all reduce a state's soft power.

Nye also identifies a strategy that balances hard and soft power, smart power, where both force and persuasion are used together to achieve the desired outcome. For example, in 2015 the United States and its partners in the P5+1 (the five permanent members of the UN Security Council, plus Germany) used soft power and hard power when dealing with Iran. They used a combination of economic sanctions, the threat of possible military action (hard power) and a diplomatic process to secure a deal with Iran to reduce its nuclear weapons programme.

These types of power can be thought of as a spectrum of options, ranging from very forceful actions (such as military force); to a mix of soft power diplomacy and hard power sanctions (smart power); to sophisticated soft power communications campaigns designed to persuade and attract. All of the forms of power – military, economic, structural, relational – that are described in this section can be used as tactics in this spectrum.

Hard	Smart	Soft
Military force, Sanctions	Payment, Diplomacy, Trade/Aid	Outreach, Cultural ties

Figure 1.1 *Hard to soft power scale*

Hard power	Smart power	Soft power
Military action taken against Islamic State in Syria and Iraq by US and others in 2014. Soft or smart power options were not possible with Islamic State, which was not prepared to negotiate. Military force against Saddam Hussein in 2003 by the US coalition. Critics of the invasion have said that UN weapons inspectors should have been given more time and that a smart power approach was possible (combining inspections with the threat of military force).	The nuclear deal signed between Iran and P5+1 in July 2015. The P5+1 used a combination of tactics: diplomatic negotiations, economic sanctions and an unstated but possible threat of military force. *Foreign Affairs* magazine praised this as a 'textbook example of successfully conceived and implemented foreign policy'. Violent protest groups such as Hezbollah not only use hard power against their adversaries, but also build and run schools, establish and maintain health care facilities, and participate in democratic coalition politics in the Lebanese parliament.	Development aid plays a huge part in powerful states trying to achieve their outcomes through persuasion. The United States state aid agency (USAID) gives most aid to countries where development matters for US security interests. In 2015, Afghanistan and Pakistan received the most US aid (see page vii for 'development' explanation). China has pledged up to $1.4 trillion in infrastructure investment in Africa. In return, China has favourable access to natural resources from African states.

Subject vocabulary

hard power achieving aims through force

soft power achieving aims through persuasion or influence

smart power achieving aims through force, persuasion and influence

sanctions official orders or laws stopping trade or communication with another state, as a way of forcing its leaders to make political changes

General vocabulary

persuasion making someone decide to do something, especially by giving them reasons why they should do it, or asking them many times to do it

ethical relating to principles of what is right and wrong

exemplary excellent and providing a good example for people to follow

rule of law a situation in which everyone in a country is expected to obey the laws, including the government, powerful people and military leaders

annexation taking control of a country or area next to your own, especially by using force

spectrum a complete range of opinions, people or situations going from one extreme to its opposite

aid help, such as money or food, given by an organization or government to a country or to people who are in a difficult situation

negotiation official discussions between the representatives of opposing groups who are trying to reach an agreement, especially in business or politics

infrastructure the basic systems and structures that a state or organization needs in order to work properly, for example roads, railways or banks

Synonyms

sophisticated .. advanced, developed

investment .... money

Definitions with audio
Click on highlighted terms to see the definition and hear the audio.

Vocabulary lists
Select the icons at the back of the book to see complete vocabulary lists.

Command terms

Analyse ....Break down in order to bring out the essential elements or structure.

Compare ....Give an account of the similarities between two (or more) items or situations, referring to both (all) of them throughout.

Compare and
contrast................Give an account of similarities and differences between two (or more) items or situations, referring to both (all) of them throughout.

Contrast...............Give an account of the differences between two (or more) items or situations, referring to both (all) of them throughout.

Define ....Give the precise meaning of a word, phrase, concept or physical quantity.

Describe ....Give a detailed account.

Discuss ....Offer a considered and balanced review that includes a range of arguments, factors or hypotheses. Opinions or conclusions should be presented clearly and supported by appropriate evidence.

Distinguish..........Make clear the differences between two or more concepts or items.

Evaluate...............Make an appraisal by weighing up the strengths and limitations.

Examine...............Consider an argument or concept in a way that uncovers the assumptions and interrelationships of the issue.

Explain ....Give a detailed account including reasons or causes.

Identify ....Provide an answer from a number of possibilities.

Justify....................Give valid reasons or evidence to support an answer or conclusion.

Outline.................Give a brief account or summary.

Suggest.................Propose a solution, hypothesis or other possible answer.

To what extent...Consider the merits or otherwise of an argument or concept. Opinions and conclusions should be presented clearly and supported with appropriate evidence and sound argument.

Discussion activity

These cartoons about interdependence, human rights, development, and conflict are helpful in starting the conversation about global politics. When looking at interdependence, you can brainstorm about the different ways nations depend on each other for survival and security. Human rights are supposed to be universal; however, can you think of human rights that might be culturally relative? Development is often thought to raise the standards of living, but are there negative by-products to the processes of development? When looking at conflict, can you think of specific examples of non-violent and violent conflicts?

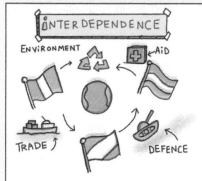

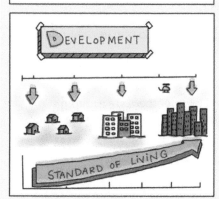

1 Power, sovereignty and international relations

1.1 Key concept: Power

Key idea:
Power is the ability to influence other groups in global politics and achieve outcomes.

What is power?

There is no single agreed definition of power (see page vi for 'power' explanation). But at its simplest, power is about achieving desired goals and influencing others. All groups and individuals in global politics have different amounts and types of power, and feel the effects of their power, or lack of power. States can be divided into powerful, less powerful and **fragile** states. States may be powerful in different ways, for example economically but not militarily. International organizations, such as the United Nations and the European Union, have power. **Multinational** companies (MNCs) – some wealthier than states – non-governmental organizations (NGOs) and **terrorist** groups all use power to achieve their desired goals.

Power can be used to achieve **material** gains. For example, a state may want to use its power to agree a trade deal or defeat a terrorist group. It may also be used to persuade others to **conform** to a political or economic idea. For example, a state may use its power to persuade other states to choose a **democratic**, capitalist model of government or to fight **corruption**. A terrorist group might use its power to **radicalize** others to support an extremist **ideology**.

Power is not fixed. States can become more powerful, whilst others see their power decline. Non-state groups can be powerful and cause problems for established state powers. Through **intergovernmental organizations** (IGOs), smaller states can cooperate with other states to become more powerful than they would be alone. For example, members of a **military alliance** such as NATO may respond collectively to security threats by launching military action. The kind of response that actors in global politics choose to use can enable others to draw conclusions about their power. Similarly, political and economic unions, such as the European Union, may establish a single currency zone that aims to maximize their economic power.

Power gives groups involved in world politics the ability to **pursue** their **interests**, whatever these interests may be at any given time.

Articulation sentences:
There is no agreed definition of power. However there are economic, military, political and other forms of power, and it can be used to achieve a state or group's interests.

Types of power

Hard, soft and smart

Tactically, states and other groups in global politics can choose to force or persuade others to do what they would like. Joseph Nye, a Harvard professor of international relations, describes these tactics as **hard power** and **soft power**.

With hard power, a state or group tries to achieve its aims through **coercion**. State A will force State B to do what it wants. State B will be aware that it is being forced to do what State A wants and will usually be less powerful than State A.

General vocabulary

fragile weak or uncertain, and likely to become worse under pressure

terrorist someone who uses violence such as bombing or shooting to obtain political demands

material relating to your money, possessions and living conditions, rather than the needs of your mind or soul

corruption dishonest, illegal or immoral behaviour, especially from someone with power

radicalize make people accept new and often extreme ideas, especially ideas about complete social and political change

pursue continue doing an activity or trying to achieve something over a long period of time

interests the things that bring advantages to someone or something

tactically related to smaller scale actions that you do to achieve what you want, especially as part of a game or large plan

Subject vocabulary

multinational operating in more than one country

democratic a system of government in which the population chooses those who govern them, through free and fair elections

ideology opinions or beliefs, often linked to a particular political system or culture

intergovernmental between or involving governments of different countries

intergovernmental organizations organizations composed primarily of sovereign states (referred to as member states)

military alliance a relationship or cooperation between states that are committed to using their armed forces in supporting similar military objectives

Synonyms

conform .... obey

coercion .... force

With soft power, a state or group tries to achieve its aims through **persuasion** or influence. State A will persuade State B to do what it wants, with or without State B being aware that this is what State A wants. Nye describes this as 'the power to get others to want what you want'. States and groups that use soft power can use culture, foreign policy (if **ethical** and **exemplary**) and political values (for example democracy, **rule of law**, tolerance, justice) to persuade other states (see page vi for 'justice' explanation). An unpopular or unethical foreign policy (such as the 2003 invasion of Iraq or the 2014 **annexation** of Crimea) or a lack of political freedom at home (such as in China) may all reduce a state's soft power.

Nye also identifies a strategy that balances hard and soft power, smart power, where both force and persuasion are used together to achieve the desired outcome. For example, in 2015 the United States and its partners in the P5+1 (the five permanent members of the UN Security Council, plus Germany) used soft power and hard power when dealing with Iran. They used a combination of economic **sanctions**, the threat of possible military action (hard power) and a diplomatic process to secure a deal with Iran to reduce its nuclear weapons programme.

These types of power can be thought of as a **spectrum** of options, ranging from very forceful actions (such as military force); to a mix of soft power diplomacy and hard power sanctions (smart power); to sophisticated soft power communications campaigns designed to persuade and attract. All of the forms of power – military, economic, structural, relational – that are described in this section can be used as tactics in this spectrum.

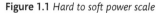

Hard	Smart	Soft
Military force, Sanctions	Payment, Diplomacy, Trade/Aid	Outreach, Cultural ties

Figure 1.1 *Hard to soft power scale*

Hard power	Smart power	Soft power
Military action taken against Islamic State in Syria and Iraq by US and others in 2014. Soft or smart power options were not possible with Islamic State, which was not prepared to negotiate. Military force against Saddam Hussein in 2003 by the US coalition. Critics of the invasion have said that UN weapons inspectors should have been given more time and that a smart power approach was possible (combining inspections with the threat of military force).	The nuclear deal signed between Iran and P5+1 in July 2015. The P5+1 used a combination of tactics: diplomatic **negotiations**, economic sanctions and an unstated but possible threat of military force. *Foreign Affairs* magazine praised this as a 'textbook example of successfully conceived and implemented foreign policy'. Violent protest groups such as Hezbollah not only use hard power against their adversaries, but also build and run schools, establish and maintain health care facilities, and participate in democratic coalition politics in the Lebanese parliament.	Development **aid** plays a huge part in powerful states trying to achieve their outcomes through persuasion. The United States state aid agency (USAID) gives most aid to countries where development matters for US security interests. In 2015, Afghanistan and Pakistan received the most US aid (see page vii for 'development' explanation). China has pledged up to $1.4 trillion in **infrastructure** **investment** in Africa. In return, China has favourable access to natural resources from African states.

Subject vocabulary

hard power achieving aims through force

soft power achieving aims through persuasion or influence

smart power achieving aims through force, persuasion and influence

sanctions official orders or laws stopping trade or communication with another state, as a way of forcing its leaders to make political changes

General vocabulary

persuasion making someone decide to do something, especially by giving them reasons why they should do it, or asking them many times to do it

ethical relating to principles of what is right and wrong

exemplary excellent and providing a good example for people to follow

rule of law a situation in which everyone in a country is expected to obey the laws, including the government, powerful people and military leaders

annexation taking control of a country or area next to your own, especially by using force

spectrum a complete range of opinions, people or situations going from one extreme to its opposite

aid help, such as money or food, given by an organization or government to a country or to people who are in a difficult situation

negotiation official discussions between the representatives of opposing groups who are trying to reach an agreement, especially in business or politics

infrastructure the basic systems and structures that a state or organization needs in order to work properly, for example roads, railways or banks

Synonyms

sophisticated .. advanced, developed

investment .... money

Hard power	Smart power	Soft power
Military force was used against the Gaddafi regime in Libya in 2011, with a NATO air campaign authorized by the UN Security Council to protect civilians. However, the Obama administration was initially reluctant to use military force, focusing instead on withdrawing troops from Iraq and Afghanistan. During Obama's presidency, there was reluctance to deploy soldiers to new conflicts.	President Obama's speech in Cairo in 2009 pledged to reset relations with the Muslim world in the Middle East. However, this public message was combined with a continuation of military force in Iraq and Afghanistan. The US administration attempted to achieve a decisive outcome before withdrawing US troops in 2011 and 2014.	Natural disasters ranging from the South Asian tsunami in 2005; the Haiti earthquake in 2009; and the West African Ebola outbreak in 2014–15 have seen huge donations from states and even the deployment of troops to help. Sporting events such as the London and Sochi Olympic Games in 2012 and 2014 can be used to boost a state's global image.

 Articulation sentences:
Hard power relies on force, whereas soft power involves the use of persuasion. Smart power is the combination of both of these tactics.

Challenges of soft power

Supporters of soft power argue that governments that have liberal values and practices may provide an attractive example to some people in states and societies that may lack democratic institutions. They may be attracted to democratic politics, economic systems based on freedom and choice, support for human rights, and other generally accepted standards and right for individuals (see page vi for 'human rights' explanation).

However, consistency and patience is needed. Soft power can take years to create, but may be lost in an instant or in a single image. For example, photographs of US soldiers mistreating prisoners in Abu Ghraib prison in Iraq in 2003 became synonymous with a military campaign that many people considered illegitimate and illegal. Trust and credibility are essential if states and groups want to use soft power in order to persuade.

Soft power is also hard to use because cultures and values are embedded in society, and are therefore outside a government's control. States may also want to communicate different messages to different audiences through soft power; what persuades in Paris may not persuade in Damascus.

 Articulation sentence:
Soft power is fragile – it can easily be destroyed – and it is often embedded in society and not within a government's control.

Military power

Military power is essential when using hard power. Military resources (land, air or sea) are the ultimate means to force another group or state to comply or to change their behaviour. The most powerful states are often thought to be those with the largest armies, the most advanced weapons (including nuclear weapons), and the technology and willingness to use their military power against one or more targets.

It is possible to compare and measure the military resources available to states. We can look at the number of soldiers, the amount spent on defence, or the amount spent as a percentage of a state's **GDP**. As of 2015, *The Economist* estimated each of these as follows.

General vocabulary

GDP Gross Domestic Product: the total value of all goods and services produced in a country, in one year, except for income received from abroad

budgets the money that is available to an organization or person

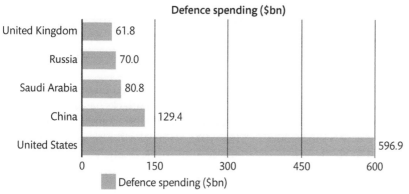

Figure 1.2 *States' defence spending in $billion graph*

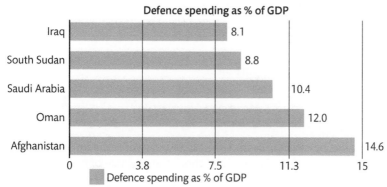

Figure 1.3 *States' defence spending as % of GDP graph*

States	Armed forces (by 1,000)
1. China	2,333
2. United States	1,433
3. India	1,346
4. North Korea	1,190
5. Russia	771

These data allow analysts to make different conclusions about military power. Poor but unstable states such as Afghanistan, South Sudan and Iraq have to spend a high proportion of their GDP on defence. They remain focused on their domestic instability and do not show any military power ambitions beyond reducing internal threats. States with large populations, such as China, the United States and India, unsurprisingly, have large numbers of troops (larger than the populations of some states). Wealthy countries and those keen to play a global role in security spend the most on defence, with four of the UN Security Council members (US, China, Russia and the UK) having the largest defence **budgets** in the world.

But it is dangerous to draw firm conclusions about military power from statistics about resources alone. What matters is whether military resources are actually used and whether they are successful when they are used. Success should be measured by whether the stated objectives of the use of military power are, in reality, achieved.

Synonyms

unstable .... insecure

firm .... fixed

Is the War on Terror a successful use of military power?

- The United States has impressive military resources but failed to achieve a decisive victory in Afghanistan and Iraq. These campaigns cost at least $1.6 trillion and lasted 13 years in Afghanistan and 8 years in Iraq.

- In 2013, the United States and its allies resumed military action in Iraq to **counter** a new threat from Islamic State. During the 2003–2011 war in Iraq, the United States' superior military technology was severely tested by **insurgency** tactics and the use of far less **sophisticated** technology by armed opposition groups, such as roadside bombs.

- Campaigns in Iraq and Afghanistan were part of a so-called War on Terror, launched in 2001. Since then, the number of terrorist attacks has increased and dangerous insurgencies have spread. From Afghanistan and Iraq they have spread across the Middle East (to Syria), across North Africa (to Libya and Tunisia) and to South Asia. Pakistan has seen the most dramatic rise in terrorist-related violence since 2001.

 Articulation sentences:

Military power is often measured by the size of a state's military or its military spending. It is also useful to assess how effective a state's military is in the conflicts that it engages in.

Is military power declining in importance?

Military power less useful and significant	Military power still useful and significant
Military power has been unsuccessful in many major conflicts since 2001 (Afghanistan, Iraq, Libya). It does not work against contemporary non-state actors or armed opposition groups.	Military power is still important to check the advance of non-state groups such as Islamic State who threaten state sovereignty (see page vi for 'sovereignty' explanation).
Inter-state war is decreasing, military conflict between states is nearly non-existent (see page vii for 'conflict' explanation). Conventional armies deployed against states are outdated.	Intra-state war is increasing. The world faces complex threats from civil war and insurgencies which pose a global security threat. Inter-state war has not disappeared completely. Conflict between Russia and Ukraine (2014) demonstrates a continuing threat.
Increasing public and political reluctance for Western troops to be deployed, making it difficult to find support and legitimacy for military action.	Military force is still useful to protect civilians (Libya, 2011) under the **doctrine** of Responsibility to Protect.

Military power and soft power

Military power is not just used to force other groups into action. It is frequently used for **humanitarian** objectives and to prevent human suffering in the **aftermath** of natural disasters. For example:

- In 2014, the United States, France and the United Kingdom sent troops to Liberia, Guinea and Sierra Leone to help tackle the Ebola crisis.

- Troops were sent to Haiti in 2009 to help deal with the earthquake, and to South Asia in 2005 to help deal with the tsunami.

Militant groups often respond to humanitarian disasters, too. For example, after the Pakistan floods of 2011, the Pakistani Taliban **sought** to increase their soft power by launching their own **relief** operations.

General vocabulary

counter do something in order to prevent something bad from happening or to reduce its bad effects

insurgency an attempt by a group of people to take control of their government using force and violence

civil war a war in which opposing groups of people from the same country fight each other in order to gain political control

humanitarian concerned with improving bad living conditions and preventing human suffering

aftermath the period of time after something such as a war, storm or accident when people are still dealing with the results

militant groups non-state armed groups that are willing to use strong or violent action in order to achieve political or social change

relief money, food, clothes and so on given to people who are poor or hungry

Synonyms

sophisticated .. advanced, developed

doctrine .... belief

sought .... tried

CHALLENGE YOURSELF

 Thinking and Research skills

Research Russia's military intervention in Ukraine in 2014. What was Russia aiming to achieve? Were they successful? Using this example, and any others you feel are relevant, write an answer to the question 'Is military power declining in importance?'

Military power is used less against other states than previously in history, and is now primarily used against non-state actors or intra-state threats.

Economic power

As with military power, there are several ways to measure a state's economic power. These can also be used to measure its development, as is explained further in Unit 3: Development (page 48).

Method	Explanation
Gross Domestic Product	Measures merely the size of domestic output, for example in billions of dollars. Some analysts expect China to overtake the United States on this measure in the next decade.
Gross Domestic Product per person	Measures the size of the economy as a proportion of the total population. By this measure, analysts expect China to take much longer to overtake the United States. They see this as evidence that the benefits of economic growth are not spread as widely amongst the population as in the United States.
Economic growth percentage	Measures the annual or quarterly percentage by which a state's economy has grown (or decreased).

It is possible for states to seek only economic power. Japan and Germany have large economies. However, since the end of the Second World War they have chosen to pursue economic power only and to not seek to increase their military power. They have small armed forces, which they use rarely, and only as a part of international coalitions.

But it is unlikely that a state will be a significant military power if it is not also a significant economic power. All the members of the UN Security Council are large economic powers, especially the United States and China. Economically weaker countries, such as those in Figure 1.3 (page 5), have to spend a higher proportion of their GDP in order to attempt to build effective militaries.

States can use economic power as a form of hard power. States frequently impose sanctions on other states to force them to change their behaviour. For example, tough sanctions were placed on the Iranian economy by the United States and European Union in order to force Iran to negotiate a deal to reduce its nuclear weapons programme. In 2012, Iran's currency collapsed. *The Economist* estimated that GDP fell by 5.8 per cent that year, inflation rose to 50 per cent, incomes fell by 40 per cent and 50 per cent in the private sector and public sector respectively, and oil exports decreased by 50 per cent.

It is also possible for states to develop an economic relationship that balances out each state's economic strengths and weaknesses. China depends on natural resources from Africa to fuel its large population and territory. In return, African countries receive much needed investment in infrastructure from China's rich foreign exchange reserves, earned from its large export market.

Articulation sentences:
Economic power can be measured in different ways. It can be used as a method of hard power – in the form of sanctions – and is needed if states wish to be strong military powers.

General vocabulary

overtake develop or increase more quickly than someone or something else and become more successful, more important or more advanced than them

coalitions groups of states who join together to achieve a particular purpose, usually a political one

inflation a continuing increase in prices, or the rate at which prices increase

dependent needing someone or something in order to exist, be successful or be healthy

reserves supply of something kept to be used if it is needed

Synonyms

measure .... way of judging

Subject vocabulary

private sector the industries and services in a country that are owned and run by private companies, and not by the government

public sector the industries and services in a country that are owned and run by the government

Structural power

Structural power is when states influence the political ideas, structure and frameworks of global politics itself. For example, some states may wish to push others towards a more democratic, capitalist, free market economic model. The ideological struggle between capitalist and communist models of economic development is the most powerful example of this in recent history. The dominance of the capitalist model was largely achieved through a mix of hard power and the attractiveness of its economic success.

More recently, Western powers have tried to remove authoritarian regimes and build up democratic models of government. In Iraq, Afghanistan and Libya, this was attempted through the use of hard military power and regime change, with mixed results. The Arab Uprisings, which began in 2011, were driven by large popular demonstrations and the hope of a more democratic Middle East and North Africa. In general, the uprisings have failed to achieve this.

Articulation sentence:
> Structural power is the means by which states affect global politics, usually by promoting a model of politics that they favour, such as democracy or capitalism.

Relational power

Relational power is when a state has a relationship with another state and uses this relationship to influence the other state to change its behaviour. A state may use military, economic, hard, soft, smart power or a combination of all of these to achieve its aims. To be successful, the state will need to have an effective strategy. It must know the other state's strengths and weaknesses and know both what would be a convincing threat and what would be an attractive reward.

Nye identifies three types of relational power:

- Threats and rewards – that are likely to encourage the state to reach the desired goal.
- Controlling the agenda – limiting the choices of the other state in order to reach the desired goals.
- Establishing preferences – getting the other state to want the same goals as your state.

Articulation sentence:
> One state can use its influence to change the behaviour of another state, using hard, soft and smart power; this is called relational power.

Social and cultural power

Globalization has made it possible for some countries to export their cultural resources across the world (see page vii for 'globalization' explanation). Global brands such as *The Simpsons*, Facebook, the BBC, Real Madrid, Apple and Samsung have become almost universally known and popular. It is difficult to know whether this brand popularity has any soft power benefit for the countries from which the brand originates. For example, opinion polls in Pakistan show that the BBC World Service is popular. However, this does not necessarily mean that the United Kingdom is also perceived positively. Therefore, cultural power connects diverse populations around the world at a more human, rather than state strategic, level.

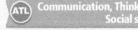

Cyber power

The cyber revolution has created an entirely new way for political groups to try to influence others. The internet has **empowered** new groups both at a state and individual level. These include organizations, such as Wikileaks, which **leaked** large volumes of secret United States government diplomatic information. Nation states now invest in cyber security and have accused each other of launching cyber attacks on others. Private individuals have also been empowered and have launched cyber attacks against governments and multinational corporations. Others have launched legitimate campaigns challenging state power, such as those seen through powerful blogs during the Arab Uprisings in 2011. With key infrastructure such as banking, water, transport and telecommunications dependent on cyber security, a new battleground has opened up.

 Articulation sentences:
The relatively new social, cultural and cyber powers have varying effectiveness. Cultural power may do little for nation states, whereas cyber power has empowered many groups, states and individuals.

General vocabulary

empowered giving someone more control over their own life or situation

leaked deliberately gave secret information to a media company such as a newspaper

frustrate prevent someone's plans, efforts or attempts from succeeding

order the political, social or economic situation at a particular time

Economic power	Structural power	Relational power	Social, cultural and cyber power
Sought by Japan and Germany since the end of the Second World War; necessary for military power	Impact on the global political framework is achieved – usually by promoting a preferred political model e.g. democracy	One state influencing the behaviour of another state	Social and cultural power connects populations but impacts less than cyber power e.g. Wikileaks

Measuring power

Taking all of these types of power into account, a judgement can be made about how powerful or weak a state is. We can also establish whether a state's power is increasing or declining.

Measuring power as resources

Power can be measured by calculating the size of, for example, armies, economies and populations. Critics of this way of measuring power say that this is not helpful because it does not take into account what states actually *do* with these resources. States may be reluctant or unable to use their power resources, even if these resources are considerable. States may misuse their power resources and make strategic mistakes. States may face opponents who seem less powerful, but still have the **capacity** to **frustrate**, resist or even defeat their power.

Measuring power as behavioural outcomes

Measuring the practical effect that states have when they use their power resources is another way of assessing power. This involves a judgement about whether, for example, **air strikes** or economic sanctions have achieved the desired effect and whether they have changed the behaviour of the other state in the way that was intended.

Distribution of power

Power can also be understood by looking at world politics as a whole. Is the world **order unipolar**, with one state clearly more powerful than all of the others and able to achieve its objectives without resistance? Is power spread around equally between lots of powerful states and non-state groups in a **multipolar** system where many states compete with each other? Is there a **bipolar** system, in which two rival but equally powerful states are in conflict with each other, perhaps making both reluctant to challenge the other?

Synonyms

capacity .... ability

Subject vocabulary

air strikes attacks in which military aircraft drop bombs

unipolar when one state is more powerful than all the others

multipolar when many states are powerful and compete with each other

bipolar when two states are equally powerful, and the main competition is between these two powers and not others

Country X

Country Y   Country Z

Figure 1.4a *Unipolar world order*   **Figure 1.4b** *Bipolar system*

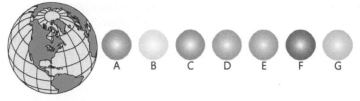

Figure 1.4c *Multipolar system*

The distribution of power in global politics at any given time is an indicator of global stability. An imbalance of power amongst groups can often mean that war or conflict is more likely. This is because states or other groups may feel that they have enough power to use force to achieve their aims, or that an adversary is becoming too powerful and thus needs to have their capabilities and influence reduced. It is possible to achieve a relative balance of power. For example, during the Cold War, the balance of power between the United States and the Soviet Union prevented both countries from beginning full-scale military hostilities against each other. However, the period was extremely volatile: both states increased their military (especially nuclear weapons) resources and the possibility of conflict remained very real. A balance of power amongst states and other global groups contributes to the establishment of an orderly international society.

See Unit 4: Peace and conflict (pages 64–82) for an explanation of how the distribution of power affects peace and stability in the global world order (see page vii for 'peace' explanation).

 Articulation sentences:

Power can be measured by assessing the size of a state's resources, or by measuring how effective a state is in achieving its objectives. Distribution of power between world states can also be used to measure global stability.

Theories of power

Realism

Realists explain power politics largely in terms of states' hard power capabilities. They see states as locked in competition with each other. Each state wants to protect its national security (both military and economic) against threats from other states in an anarchic world order. According to realism, states either pursue offensive realism, where they aim to *expand* their global power; or defensive realism, where they aim merely to *defend* themselves against external threats and maintain the status quo. A key theorist of realism as it relates to power is John Mearsheimer. His 2001 book, *The Tragedy of Great Power Politics*, proposed that states compete with each other to gain power at the expense of others and to make sure that they do not lose power.

Liberalism

Liberals, in contrast, believe that soft power, co-operation and a rules based international order are the most effective and safest way of using power in global politics. Examples of soft power include leading by example, **consensus** building and the establishment of opportunities for cooperation. Liberals see states as more powerful when they work together, for example through cooperation in international organizations. They believe that states should use power by conforming to a world order governed by **international law** and respecting human rights. They see power as distributed amongst a wide range of groups and processes, from international organizations (such as the United Nations) to international trade and communications.

The table below summarizes some of the different theoretical approaches to power.

Theoretical approach	Perspectives on power
Realism	Military power, economic sanctions and incentives.
Liberalism	International institutions, international law, human rights and global trade.

Articulation sentence:

Realists believe states use hard power to gain and maintain power for their own ends, whereas liberals believe that soft power, combined with international cooperation, is the best method of operating in world politics.

Power transition

Power is not a fixed concept. States can become more powerful. For example, a successful economic strategy may deliver a sustained period of economic growth, or a state may achieve military success. This increases a state's power and credibility, and also other states' fear that it may use military force again. States can also become less powerful. For example, an economic crisis or an unsuccessful conflict may damage a state's credibility and the perceived competence of its armed forces.

Rising powers

Much attention has been given to the economic rise of China and the so-called BRIC countries, comprising Brazil, Russia, India and China. All of these countries achieved remarkable economic growth between 2001 and 2011. In 2008, there was a global financial crisis, and growth for these countries slowed dramatically between 2010 and 2014 (see graph below). The type of power enjoyed by the BRIC economies remains predominantly economic and has been vulnerable to economic slowdown. The Russian economy, in particular, suffered a severe **recession** and suffered further when economic sanctions were imposed on it in 2014 after the Ukraine crisis.

Average annual growth rates for BRICS and three major developed economies

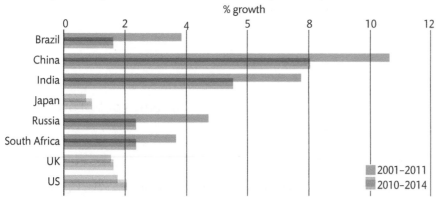

Source: Calculated from IMF World Economic Outlook Database October 2014

Figure 1.5 *Growth rate of BRICS graph (including South Africa, which joined in 2010)*

Declining powers

Many ask whether the United States is a world superpower in decline. The global financial crisis of 2008 exposed weaknesses in the US economy and started a long economic recession. Military failure in Iraq and Afghanistan made the Obama administration reluctant to use its military power in future conflicts. The United States did not want to use military force against the Syrian Assad regime in 2013. This was despite the fact that it had previously said that any use of chemical weapons by the Assad regime would be considered a 'red line', meaning that force would be used against the government.

Regarding the United Nations Security Council, many question whether the United Kingdom and France are still powerful enough to deserve permanent member status. There have been debates in the United Kingdom about military intervention in Syria against Islamic State (in 2015) and whether to upgrade the UK's Trident nuclear weapons system. These debates are as much about the willingness and ability to project the UK's power and influence on the global stage as they are about the merits of the individual decisions themselves.

Power diffusion

A key power change in global politics has been the increasing power of terrorist non-state groups. Violent groups such as Islamic State, Boko Haram, al-Shabaab and al-Qaeda have gained considerable power. They have been able to launch deadly terrorist attacks against New York and Washington on 11 September 2001. They have been able to gain control of large amounts of territory from sovereign states in Nigeria, Iraq, Afghanistan and Syria. They have recruited foreign fighters using online networks. Most of these groups have shown no interest in negotiation with other actors. Consequently, for states whose security is put at risk, hard power solutions are the only option to counter the security threat posed by these groups.

To some extent, globalization has put greater power in the hands of the individual. The Arab Uprisings of 2011 spread so quickly because protesters were able to see on blogs and global television networks, such as al-Jazeera, what was happening in other parts of the Middle East and North Africa. They were inspired to join the uprisings. However, despite these popular uprisings, the power of nation-state governments has proven to be more enduring. Governments have been able to resist popular pressure (for example, in Syria) and take measures to stop further rebellion (as seen in the return to military rule in Egypt).

> **Articulation sentence:**
> Power is a fluid concept, with some nations gaining it, some losing it and others having their power diffused by the rise of militant non-state groups.

1.2 Key concept: Sovereignty

Key idea:

States are sovereign when they exercise **supreme** control over what happens inside their borders.

What is sovereignty?

Sovereignty is defined as a state's ability to rule itself. States are sovereign when they have full control and authority over what happens inside their borders. Sovereignty is an essential principle in global politics. States should respect the

Subject vocabulary

diffused spread amongst a number of different global political actors

General vocabulary

supreme having the highest position of power, importance or influence

sovereignty of other states, as well as maintain and defend their own sovereignty. International organizations, such as the United Nations, base their rules on respect for state sovereignty.

Sovereignty can be thought of as internal and external.

Internal sovereignty is about states governing themselves independently. States have full responsibility for, and power over, what happens within their borders. For example, they can decide and enforce their own laws, collect taxes, and spend the money raised on their own priorities and needs. States can decide their own trade policies, perhaps by placing tariffs on imports or deciding to join regional free trade areas with no tariff barriers.

External sovereignty is about how states interact externally with other states and international organizations. States generally respect each other's borders and do not intervene or interfere in what goes on within the borders of those states. States may make representations on other states' internal actions by way of established intergovernmental bodies, such as the United Nations.

Articulation sentence:

A state with sovereignty has complete control over its own government and it has external sovereignty when it allows other states control over what happens within their borders.

State sovereignty and legitimacy

A state's sovereignty is dependent on other states recognizing the state as a state. The idea of sovereignty comes from classical Rome and medieval Europe. The Treaty of Westphalia in 1648 can be seen as the point when the ideas of statehood were formally established. The principle of sovereignty has been supported through putting ideas such as diplomacy and non-intervention into practice.

Groups such as Islamic State may call themselves a state, but if no other states or international organizations recognize them, they cannot be considered a sovereign state. International legitimacy is essential in order for a state to be considered an independent sovereign country. That said, organizations that are not sovereign states can display many of the features outlined in the 1933 Montevideo Convention. The convention outlined the following aspects of a state and is still a useful guide to the features of sovereign nation states. Sovereign states should have:

- a permanent population;
- a defined territory and borders;
- effective government;
- the capacity and legitimacy to enter into relations with other states (see page vi for 'legitimacy' explanation).

For example, the European Union has a single currency, a flag, a parliament and a central bank. It also has a defined external border and the internal borders between its member states are largely irrelevant. It has a foreign policy and is increasingly entering into relations with other states through its High Representative for Foreign Affairs. The EU is not an independent single nation state, but has such deep levels of cooperation and integration that it does have many of the identifying features of independent states.

This table includes the key features and indicators of sovereign states. It also includes the challenges of identifying sovereignty. In some states that are still sovereign independent states, some of these features may be contested or in doubt.

Subject vocabulary

internal sovereignty the ability of a state to exert legitimate control over its population and manage its affairs independently

tariffs taxes on goods coming into or going out of a country

external sovereignty when states are recognized as independent and sovereign by other states, and are not interfered with; also their external border is respected

Synonyms

enforce	....	make people obey
interact	....	work together
intervene	......	get involved
outlined	....	described
defined	....	clear

General vocabulary

interfere deliberately get involved in a situation where you are not wanted or needed

recognize officially accept that an organization, a government or document has legal or official authority

contested where there is lack of agreement on what a concept or idea means

Equally, some non-state groups that are not sovereign states may share some of the features and functions of nation states, challenging states' sovereignty.

Feature	Indicator	Problems of identifying
Permanent population	Identifying whether people live in a permanent place, or whether the population is less fixed, such as refugees.	Refugees. A sovereign state may suffer an insurgency, such as in Iraq and Syria, leading to refugees fleeing the country. In this sense, the population is no longer permanent, but it is still a sovereign state.
Defined territory	Identifying territorial borders through maps; decisions of the International Court of Justice and international law which agree state borders, or say when these borders are in dispute.	Many borders are disputed between nation states. For example, between Israel and the Palestinian Territories or in the Kashmir region between India and Pakistan. Non-state groups are increasingly taking control of territory from nation states. In 2014, Islamic State declared that it had established a caliphate across both Syria and Iraq. The border between the two countries became increasingly irrelevant even if, in international law, the border still exists.
Effective government	Identifying whether a government exists and whether it has full authority and control over the state's territory.	Fragile states, such as Somalia and the Democratic Republic of Congo, do not have effective governments that have authority across the whole of the country. However, they are still recognized sovereign states. The European Union is often criticized for acting like a state, with the power to create laws and force member states to comply, even though it is not a sovereign state. In 2015, Islamic State was called a pseudo-state by some analysts. They added that it had an effective – if illegitimate – form of government, able to collect revenue, manage oil fields and control territory.
Capacity to enter relations with other states	Tracking diplomatic relations between states through international summits, membership of international organizations, or bilateral and multilateral partnerships.	Regions (such as Kosovo and the Palestinian Territories) that are trying to gain independence are often given a form of membership of international organizations, known as observer status. The European Union has its own High Representative for Foreign Affairs and its own overseas aid budget, which allows it to have an increasingly significant and independent voice on the world stage.

The Montevideo Convention is used to determine whether a nation is a sovereign state, however there are many challenges to this method because some non-state groups conform to some features of statehood.

Gaining recognized statehood

In modern global politics, the United Nations is the key international body which agrees the legitimacy of state borders and makes rulings on borders that are contested. Being recognized as a full member state of the United Nations is the ultimate confirmation of independent statehood. Since the United Nations was founded in 1947, the number of nation states has grown from 52 to 193 states. Most recently, South Sudan gained independence in 2011 and became a full member of the UN.

At an international level, where borders or sovereignty are disputed, the resolutions of the UN Security Council and the decisions of the International Court of Justice (ICJ) are important statements of international law. However, rulings from both institutions are still sometimes ignored or questioned by states.

At a national level, states and regions seeking independence often hold a referendum, in which the population votes directly on whether it should become independent. This is seen as the most legitimate way for new states to be recognized. In a referendum in 2014, Scotland voted against becoming an independent state, separate from the United Kingdom.

In the table are further examples of claims of, and disputes over, sovereignty.

Example	Disputes over/ justifications for sovereignty
Kosovo	In 2008, Kosovo declared its independence from the Republic of Serbia. There was not a referendum to ask the Kosovan population directly whether they wanted Kosovo to be an independent state. The United States and other Western states supported Kosovo's desire for independence. The ICJ stated that Kosovo's declaration of independence 'did not violate international law', but the UN has not declared Kosovo a full independent member state of the UN.
Crimea/ Ukraine	In 2014, the Russian Federation annexed the region of Crimea in Ukraine. A referendum was held, but the UN declared the referendum illegitimate, due to the presence of Russian troops. Russia justified its actions using the example of Kosovo's claims for independence. The UN Security Council attempted to pass a resolution declaring the referendum illegitimate, but Russia vetoed this.
South China Sea	China wants to expand its territorial waters in the South China Sea. China has said that it does not recognize the authority of the ICJ and will not comply with its decisions. In response, the United States Navy has sent warships to carry out regular 'freedom of navigation' patrols through waters that China claims as its own, but that the United States considers to be international waters.
Kashmir (India and Pakistan)	The so-called Line of Control between India and Pakistan in the contested region of Kashmir is a UN-agreed temporary border. It is designed to keep Pakistani and Indian troops apart. Both India and Pakistan claim sovereignty over the region. The Line of Control was agreed in 1972 and is monitored by UN peacekeepers. This is the UN's longest peacekeeping operation anywhere in the world.

General vocabulary

resolutions formal decisions or statements agreed on by a group of people, especially after a vote

vetoed refused to allow something to happen, by having the right to special powers which allow an actor to legitimately stop what other actors want

navigation when someone sails a ship along a river or other area of water

patrols moving military forces through an area at regular times to check that there is no trouble or danger

Subject vocabulary

referendum when people vote in order to make a decision about a particular subject, rather than voting for an individual or political party

international waters waters surrounding the globe that are not part of the territorial sea or a state's internal waters

CHALLENGE YOURSELF

 Research skills

Look at international news websites to find out about South Sudan gaining independence. What process did they use in order to gain independence? What role did the UN play in that process?

General vocabulary

occupied enter a place in a large group and keep control of it, especially by military force

settlements groups of houses and buildings where people live

prosperity when states are economically successful, generating income and managing their affairs in a way that allows individuals, businesses and the government to generate wealth

pooling sacrificing sovereignty by sharing power with other actors in global politics, most often other nation states, for example by sharing a currency (e.g. the Euro)

unilaterally done by only one of the states or groups involved in a situation

bailing out doing something to help someone out of trouble, especially financial problems

last resort the only solution after trying everything else to solve a problem

Synonyms

binding .... to be obeyed

Example	Disputes over/ justifications for sovereignty
Israel and Palestinian Territories	UN Security Council Resolution 242 was passed in 1967. It requires Israel to withdraw to the borders that existed before the 1967 Six Day War, when Israel occupied the West Bank, Golan Heights and Gaza Strip. UN Security Council resolutions are binding in international law, yet Israel has not withdrawn to the pre-1967 borders. Furthermore, it has built a security wall around, and settlements within, territory that is beyond the pre-1967 borders as agreed by the UN Security Council. Israel says that the pre-1967 borders are no longer relevant and that the security wall is needed to protect the state of Israel from terrorist attacks from Palestine.

> **Articulation sentences:**
> It is possible to gain independent statehood, usually by holding a referendum, and to become recognized by the UN. However, there are many contested states and borders around the world.

Is state sovereignty being eroded?

A common argument in global politics is that state sovereignty is being weakened by political, economic and cultural globalization. Some argue that other aspects of global politics, such as international organizations, international trade, multinational corporations and global terrorist networks, are challenging state sovereignty.

These arguments generally reflect either a liberal or a realist view of the world. For realists, states are still the most important actor in global politics, able to act independently and protect their borders. For liberals, states still exist but cooperate with each other on both economic and political matters. Liberals believe that states maximize their security and prosperity by pooling, rather than defending, their sovereignty.

Claim: State sovereignty becoming less significant	Counterclaim: State sovereignty still significant
Borders are decreasing in significance. Border checks between states are disappearing, particularly in the European Union (due to the Schengen Agreement). States are affected by issues that cross borders, for example climate change, global terrorism and migration.	Borders still define independent states. States still decide their own economic and political policies, within their borders. Some still maintain border checks. Others still act independently or unilaterally. National identity still matters, and remains a unique identifying and unifying force.
Economic globalization is reducing the economic importance of states. Many states are reducing barriers to trade and are joining trade agreements (e.g. Trans-Pacific Partnership, European Union). There is increasing freedom of movement for people and goods. Multinational corporations also have a lot of power (some are wealthier than small states), and can force states to change their economic policies in return for investment.	Economic policy (e.g. import and export tax, trade partnerships) is still decided by nation states. Multinational corporations are undoubtedly powerful, but resolving major economic crises requires action by nation states. For example, the financial crisis of 2008 was resolved by nation states and international organizations (G20, G8, International Monetary Fund). Bailing out failing multinational banks was funded by nation states as 'lenders of last resort'.

Claim: State sovereignty becoming less significant	Counterclaim: State sovereignty still significant
Intergovernmental organizations (IGOs) are becoming more numerous and more powerful. One of the most powerful organizations, the European Union, has supranational powers and can make laws and enforce them on its member states. Other IGOs recognize that states face shared challenges and try to resolve these through collective action.	States choose to join IGOs and are the key contributors to IGOs. There is no world governing body with the power to act above the nation-state level. Many IGOs allow states the right to veto and protect core national interests. Most IGOs are intergovernmental, where decisions are reached by consensus of the member states.
International conventions such as the Responsibility to Protect no longer regard state sovereignty as absolute. Instead it is conditional on states behaving responsibly. For example, external intervention by states acting unilaterally or through IGOs has been used against Afghanistan (2001), Iraq (2003), Pakistan (the operation to capture or kill Osama bin Laden, 2011), Libya (2011) and Ukraine (2014).	States can still abuse human rights or break international law with impunity. Decisions about external intervention are taken very carefully, and are dependent on international agreement. Intervention was possible in Libya (2011). However, when the Syrian government used chemical weapons (2013), there was no intervention. The majority of borders are respected by nation states. Violations by other nation states have decreased and are very rare.
Non-state actors, such as terrorist groups, are frequently challenging state sovereignty and attempting to define new borders. For example, large parts of Syria and Iraq came under the control of Islamic State (2015) and in Nigeria, Boko Haram took over parts of the country (2015).	While it is true that non-state actors are challenging state sovereignty in a number of states, this is not widespread, there remains broad international consensus about what makes a state legitimate in international law. Attempts by militant groups to seize territory are widely seen as illegitimate and often military action is launched to reassert sovereignty.

> **Articulation sentences:**
> Realists argue that despite globalization eroding state sovereignty, states are still the most powerful factors in international politics. However, liberals believe that the rise of intergovernmental organizations is becoming as important, and sometimes more important, than the role of states in the global order.

Theories of sovereignty

Realists

Realists are prepared both to defend sovereignty as an absolute, inviolable principle and to breach the sovereignty of other states if their own national interest requires it. In the first case, realists believe that state sovereignty should be protected and that the most significant actors in global politics are defined by states within sovereign state boundaries. For example, a regime in one part of the world may be run by a ruthless dictatorship that breaches the human rights of its citizens. However, the realist principle of sovereignty limits the use of force by other states to bring this dictatorship under control. This would most likely be the case if there were no national interest at stake for the realist state when considering whether or not to

General vocabulary

governing body an official organization that is responsible for making the rules for an organization, and for making sure that people follow the rules

collective shared or made by every member of a group or society

with impunity with no risk of being punished

violations actions that break a law, agreement or principle

ruthless so determined to get what you want that you do not care if you have to hurt other people in order to do it

dictatorship a country that is ruled by one person who has complete power

breaches an action that breaks a law, rule or agreement

Subject vocabulary

supranational where decisions can be taken above nation state level, usually by an organization that has the power to force nation states to conform to laws or policies

CHALLENGE YOURSELF

Thinking, Research and Self-management skills

Research the country where you live. Using the headings 'borders', 'economy', 'IGOs', 'intervention' and 'non-state groups', write a report on the sovereignty of your state. Decide whether you believe your state has maintained its sovereignty over the past 20 years or whether it is being eroded.

intervene. For example, the United States was reluctant to intervene in Rwanda in 1994 despite clear evidence that a **genocide** was taking place. On the contrary, in 2003 the United States felt it was in its national interest to launch military action against the Iraqi regime of Saddam Hussein without international approval through the United Nations.

Liberals

Liberals argue that sovereignty is an important but not exclusive principle in international political relations. Other states can be punished (for example, by the UN) if they commit crimes within their borders. For example, NATO's military intervention in Libya in 2011 was based on UN Security Council Resolution of 1973. The intervention was based in part on the principle of Responsibility to Protect (known as R2P). The Libyan government was failing in its obligation to protect civilian citizens from **mass** violence during the civil war in Libya (see page vii for 'violence' explanation).

Theoretical viewpoint	Perspective on sovereignty
Realism	Sees sovereignty as an essential feature of global politics. States are the only legitimate bodies in global politics. The interests and right of states to act independently and defend their core interests is prioritized over most other principles and ideas.
Liberalism	Sees sovereignty as one of several principles in world politics. It is important, but not always at the expense of other groups or ideas. Sovereignty is not absolute and can be pooled (with states acting together to resolve shared challenges) and challenged (when other states fail to exercise their sovereignty responsibly).

 Articulation sentence:
Liberals believe that state sovereignty is not exclusive and therefore believe in the necessity of intervention in states abusing their powers, whereas realists would argue the opposite.

How states organize themselves

States manage their internal sovereignty in different ways. **Democracy** is the most common model of state government. This means that state governments are **elected** by a free and fair process. Every member of the adult population is able to vote freely for the government or representative that they choose, without **intimidation**, interference and with every vote counting equally. Some democratic state governments **delegate** power to regions, which themselves have democratic elections, bringing decision-making closer to the people affected by those decisions. Some states run the whole country from a very powerful central government, usually in the state's capital city.

There is no single model of a democratic state. Each has its own strengths and weaknesses, each distributes power and ensures **accountability** within the state in different ways. For example, one **chamber** of the United Kingdom's Parliament, the House of Lords, is unelected. In other systems, such as the United States, the cost of running an election campaign is extremely expensive. This means that only those who can raise enough money for advertizing and campaigning stand for election. In other states, there may be a lack of political choice and very few political parties for the **electorate** to vote for.

In states that are not democracies, the governments generally need to use authoritarian means to control their territory. This means that the government is not elected or accountable to the population, and the people have no means of influencing or removing the government.

Federal states

In **federal** states, there is a government, usually in the capital city, which has central power over some policy, such as foreign policy. Beyond this, there are governments at sub-national level which have the power to make and enforce the law. For example, the United States is a federal system of government. Individual states have the power to decide and enforce their own, different laws. Some states have chosen to have the **death penalty**, whereas others do not.

Unitary states

In **unitary** states, the central government has greater control and authority over what happens within its territory. Most decisions and laws are decided by a national **legislature** such as a national elected parliament or assembly. In the United Kingdom, Scotland has its own parliament and can make its own laws in certain areas. These powers are delegated by the legislature and might, in theory, be restored back to the national parliament if necessary.

Fragile states

Fragile states may be democratic or undemocratic, but the defining feature is that the state's internal sovereignty and power is weak. The government may be non-existent, illegitimate or just too weak to have authority over its territory. For example, the civil war and insurgency in Somalia meant that the central government had no power over large parts of the country. The war prevented elections from being held and there was an almost total collapse of the government's power to keep law and order or provide **public services**, such as healthcare and education.

Authoritarian states

In states where there is no democracy, the government is not elected and governs with authority that cannot be challenged, **held to account** or influenced by the population. Leaders remain in power for as long as they wish, or until they are removed by means such as a **military coup**, foreign intervention (such as the removal of Saddam Hussein in Iraq in 2003) or popular uprising (such as the removal of Egypt's President Mubarak in 2011). In these states, human rights abuses are likely to be widespread and the rule of law is not respected.

Monarchy

Many states in Europe, Asia and the Middle East are governed by a **hereditary monarchy** or a royal family, which is unelected but has gained its authority through generations of rule by the family. Monarchies differ greatly. Some have little more than a symbolic role (such as in the United Kingdom, Sweden and Norway), while others have greater political control (such as the powerful ruling royal family in Saudi Arabia). Some monarchies have actively tried to reduce their power and to give more power to elected civilian governments, such as Morocco and the United Arab Emirates in response to the Arab Uprisings in 2011.

Theocracy

Meaning literally 'rule or government by religion', **theocracy** is where power is held by religious groups, rather than non-religious political parties. For example, the Islamic Republic of Iran is ruled by its Islamic Supreme Leader, who has the power to decide which non-religious candidates stand for election to the state's president. In Saudi Arabia, the ruling Shura Council has the power to make and enforce Saudi Arabia's Sharia or Islamic law, alongside the country's ruling monarchy.

> **Articulation sentence:**
> States can be organized in a number of different ways, ranging from democracy to autocracy and with a variety of government structures, such as federal and unitary.

CHALLENGE YOURSELF

Thinking, Communication and Social skills

What model of state government does your country use? In groups discuss whether you think this model is effective. What are the advantages and disadvantages of it?

1.3 Key concept: Interdependence

Key idea:

Interdependence is when groups in global politics rely on each other, have shared interests or have an impact on each other.

What is interdependence?

Interdependence is a key feature of a globalized world in which all groups in global politics are increasingly reliant on each other and influenced by each other (see page vi for 'interdependence' explanation).

This can be seen in a number of different ways.

- Economic interdependence. States are linked together economically because they trade with each other and the success or failure of their economies are linked. A recession in one state is likely to have an impact on that state's ability to trade with another. This can lead to the recession spreading from one state to others, as seen in the global financial crisis of 2008.
- Political interdependence. States' political decisions are likely to have an impact on other states. For example, the civil war in Syria has had a wide political impact across the Middle East, North Africa and Europe. A high number of Syrian refugees are seeking **asylum** in Europe and the regional reach of Islamic State's terrorist activities is growing in North Africa and mainland Europe (as seen in the terrorist attacks in Paris of 2015). Political instability in fragile states such as Somalia has an impact on neighbouring states, both politically and economically.
- There are a number of challenges that many states have in common, and that cannot be solved by one state on its own. For example, climate change affects all states – rich and poor – and can only be resolved through collective action, through international summits such as the Kyoto (1997), Copenhagen (2009) and the Paris climate change talks (2015).

> Articulation sentence:
> States are becoming more interdependent – economically and politically, among other ways – due to the globalization of world issues.

Intergovernmental organizations

As the world has become more globalized and states have become more interdependent, so there has been a growth in intergovernmental organizations (IGOs). These allow states to act together. States join intergovernmental organizations for a number of reasons.

- Powerful states can join IGOs in order to force or persuade other states to adopt policies or agreements that meet their national interests.
- Less powerful states can join IGOs to group together with other states. This gives them more influence than they would have if they acted alone.
- States use IGOs so that they can work together to resolve issues where acting alone is insufficient, where they need the positive actions of other states as well as their own.
- States use IGOs to increase or protect their economic or military power. They can do this through membership of a common currency (for example, the euro),

General vocabulary

asylum protection given to someone by a government because they have escaped from fighting or political trouble in their own country

by contributing to an economic IGO (such as the International Monetary Fund) or by joining a security decision-making **alliance** (such as NATO and the UN Security Council).

- States also join IGOs within regions. Regional IGOs have more united power and influence on the world stage than states in the region that act alone. Examples include the African Union, and the Association of Southeast Asian Nations (ASEAN).

 Articulation sentence:

Intergovernmental organizations provide member states with a number of benefits, such as economic strength and more influence in global politics.

Key international organizations (IGOs)

The United Nations

The United Nations (UN) is the leading international organization that is truly 'international' in nature. It has 193 member states, representing most of the world's sovereign states. Its policies are wide-ranging. Founded in 1945, it has many objectives and many different **agencies**, which it uses to achieve its four main objectives.

General vocabulary

alliance an arrangement in which two or more countries or groups agree to work together to try to change or achieve something

agencies organizations or departments, especially within a government, that do a specific job

in rotation the practice of regularly changing the person or country who does a particular job

records the facts about how successful someone or something has been in the past

Subject vocabulary

sustainable development the concept that the development needs of today's population should not result in activity that puts at risk the development needs of future generations, for example, through damage to the environment

Objectives	Agencies and activities of the UN
Promoting and protecting global peace and security	UN Security Council – passes Resolutions and authorizes peacekeeping and other military action to protect global security, under Chapter VII of the United Nations Charter. Some Resolutions authorize military action led by other international organizations, such as NATO. UN peacekeepers are sent across the world. In 2015, there were 16 UN peacekeeping operations, mostly in Africa and the Middle East.
	International Court of Justice – makes rulings in international law when states disagree over sovereignty.
Protecting and promoting human rights	UN Human Rights Council – consists of a selection of UN member states, working **in rotation**, to investigate and make other member states accountable for protecting human rights.
	UN High Commissioner for Human Rights – a UN agency that operates independently from member states. It **scrutinizes** member states' human rights' **records**.
Advancing world human and economic development	Millennium Development Goals (MDGs) – until 2015, agreed international action to promote human development across the poorest regions of the world. These were replaced by the Sustainable Development Goals (SDGs) in 2015, which continued the work of the MDGs and developed them further to focus more on **sustainable development** (see page vii for 'sustainability' explanation).
	Economic and Social Council (ECOSOC) – made up of 54 member states, serving one-year terms, ECOSOC coordinates UN action on economic, social and environmental issues. It also oversees the work of the MDGs and SDGs.
	United Nations Development Programme (UNDP) – works on UN-agreed development priorities across the world, funded by UN member states.

Synonyms

scrutinizes ..... examines carefully

Objectives	Agencies and activities of the UN
Tackling shared challenges such as climate change	The United Nations has led many important international summits on climate change. For example, the Kyoto Protocol (1997) was ratified by 59 UN member states who committed to reducing greenhouse gas emissions. Subsequent UN summits include the less successful Copenhagen Accord (signed at the 2009 UN Climate Change Conference) and the Paris Agreement (2015), which sets a path towards a legally binding global agreement on reducing climate change.

 Articulation sentence:

The United Nations is the most significant IGO, with objectives ranging from peacekeeping, to human rights protection, to economic development and climate change reduction.

Economic IGOs

Other intergovernmental organizations focus on one area, for example economic issues. The existence of economic IGOs reflects the economic interdependence of global politics and the need to:

- spread economic development and trade across the world, agreeing rules between states;
- help states when they are in financial difficulty (for example by giving loans), to avoid their economic situation getting worse and harming the world economy;
- help states with 'technical' assistance, for example advising states on how to develop their economies.

There are three main economic IGOs.

The World Trade Organization (WTO) decides and enforces the rules of international trade, and resolves trade disputes between states through negotiation. The WTO is made up of member states and is therefore an intergovernmental organization. There has to be agreement amongst all members before policy is officially adopted; everything and everyone must be in agreement. The WTO has been criticized for failing to make progress in helping developing countries to join global markets through its Doha Development Agenda. The negotiations for this began in 2001 and, as of 2015, remain in **stalemate**.

The International Monetary Fund (IMF) works to improve global cooperation on financial stability and to promote economic growth and reduce poverty across the world. Since the 1980s, the IMF has been known for forcing states to implement economic reforms in return for loans. The IMF continues to offer both financial assistance (loans) and technical advice to help states' economic development.

The World Bank focuses on states' economic development and on reducing poverty. It does this through analysing and publishing data on global economic development, and by funding development projects in less economically developed states.

 Articulation sentence:

There are a number of economic IGOs whose purpose is to prevent poverty, manage international trade regulations and promote global economic development.

Collective security

States join IGOs to improve their security. Joining together in a formal collective security alliance means that smaller states are protected by larger states, with all states pledging that an attack on one state would be treated as an attack on all member states. States agree to pool their military resources and protect each other. Acting collectively brings greater security than if states acted alone.

The North Atlantic Treaty Organization (NATO) was founded in 1949 by the United States and its western European allies in response to the Cold War threat from the Soviet Union. It is the most significant example of a formal security alliance. After the 11 September 2001 attacks, NATO used Article 5 and declared that the attacks on the United States, led by al-Qaeda, were an attack on all its member states. Subsequently, NATO led the military operations in Afghanistan against the Taliban government and al-Qaeda. NATO has expanded its membership to include many former Soviet states in Eastern Europe. Prior to the Russian annexation of Crimea in 2014, Ukraine had been in discussions about potential membership of NATO. In 2015, President Putin identified NATO as a key threat to the Russian Federation's national security.

Articulation sentence:

An IGO such as NATO exists to provide states with collective security – all member states offer one another military protection in the event of an attack.

Hybrid IGOs

As well as the United Nations, some regional IGOs have a number of different functions, ranging from economic matters (for example, shared currency or free trade agreements) to political cooperation (for example, on organized crime, climate change or migration). These are called hybrid IGOs.

The European Union (EU)

The European Union is a complex regional hybrid IGO that has a very wide range of responsibilities and supporting institutions. It has supranational powers. It was founded after the Second World War to unite former enemies, principally France and Germany. The idea was that member states would become politically and economically unified, and would become so interdependent that any future conflict would be not merely unlikely, but impossible.

Membership has grown throughout the EU's history. Most recently, a large number of former Soviet states in Eastern Europe have joined, taking the EU's membership to 28 member states. It remains an economic and political union. In 1999, the EU launched a single European currency, the euro, encouraging further integration. Not all member states use the euro, but all participate in the EU's free trade area, which allows for free movement of people, goods and services across the EU.

The EU is perhaps the world's most advanced and integrated international organization. It is sometimes criticized for acting like a nation state and for challenging state sovereignty, with the power to force member states to comply with EU law. It is made up of several key institutions, including:

- European Commission – acts as the European Union's **executive**, with the power to propose new EU laws. This part of the EU is unusual because it has the power to set the agenda of the European Union independently of the member states and to defend the core interests of the Union in its own right.

- European Parliament – the European Union is frequently criticized for having a 'democratic deficit' because its Parliament has weaker powers than the national parliaments of sovereign states.

Synonyms

collective ...... shared

deficit .... shortage

General vocabulary

executive the part of a government that makes decisions and laws

CHALLENGE YOURSELF

Research the African Union and the European Union. What are the strengths of each IGO? What are the differences between how they operate? Find out a bit about the proposed Central Asian Union. If this union was formed, what do you recommend their activities should be?

Subject vocabulary

African Union a regional IGO of which most African states are members, focusing primarily on security and economic prosperity

pandemics diseases that affect people over a very large area or the whole world

General vocabulary

biased unfairly preferring one person or group over another

governance the act of making all the decisions about taxes, laws and public services

gridlock a situation in which nothing can happen, usually because people disagree strongly

---

- European Court of Justice – has the power to force member states to comply with EU law.
- European Central Bank – the ECB has the power to set monetary policy for the member states of the EU that are in the Eurozone and have adopted the EU's single currency. Eurozone members do not have their own, independent monetary policies. Member states in the Eurozone are also required to manage their national budgets carefully and not get into debt, which could put the economic security and prosperity of the wider Eurozone at risk.

African Union (AU)

The African Union was founded in 2002, but there had previously been African regional organizations dating back to 1962. The African Union is made up of every African nation state, except Morocco, and mainly deals with security, and political and economic development. Since 2007, the AU has become more involved in peacekeeping missions in Africa, notably in Somalia, and has had considerable success. It also allows African countries to speak with one voice on the international stage. For example, in 2013, the AU threatened to withdraw from the International Criminal Court. It complained that the ICC was biased against African leaders.

Articulation sentence:
Hybrid IGOs, such as the European Union and the African Union, have military, political and economic power, providing member states with a range of benefits.

Global governance

Global governance is the way states organize themselves, make agreements and tackle shared challenges above national level, usually through international organizations with clear rules. From a liberal perspective, global governance is a key priority. It allows states to react to – and solve – problems that they have in common and that, if left unresolved, would impact on more than one state.

The growth of IGOs in recent decades might suggest that the liberal ideal of global governance is progressing well. However, international organizations are frequently limited in what they are able to agree. Often IGOs or international summits cannot agree a joint agenda for action. Realism takes over, with states protecting their national interests. Indeed, some states use their membership of IGOs precisely in order to protect their national interests. This can be seen when permanent members of the UN Security Council use their veto.

The reasons why effective global governance is difficult in modern global politics have been identified by Hale, Held and Young (2013) as:

Reason	Explanation
Multipolarity and institutional **gridlock**	Today's multipolar world has an effect on key global governance institutions. For example, the UN Security Council is more divided than it has been for many decades. Russia and China are becoming more and more powerful and are increasingly willing to use their veto power.
	The Doha Development Round at the WTO has been blocked by states' increasing defence of their core economic interests.
Harder problems and lack of consensus	The key challenges for modern global politics require action from more than one nation state. Global terrorism, climate change, fragile states and their impact on entire regions, cyber security and global pandemics require multi-state action and global consensus on what the solutions are.

The effectiveness of global governance is being challenged by states' increasing prioritization of their own interests above that of global issues, such as climate change.

Cooperation

Treaties

States do not just cooperate with each other through IGOs. A more flexible way of cooperating with other states is through bilateral and multilateral **treaties**.

- These are agreed between as many or as few states as desired.
- They may be agreed by states that group together on a particular issue, rather than by region.
- If in treaty form, they represent formal international law.
- Some treaties are used to establish, or change the rules of, international organizations.

States have to complete two stages to be fully covered by, and obliged to comply with, treaties. First, states must sign treaties. Second, most democratic states must ratify treaties that they have signed, through their national legislatures or parliaments. Some hold national referendums to give greater legitimacy to the signing of treaties.

Examples of treaties

Treaty	Objectives	Signatories	Successes and challenges
Nuclear Non-Proliferation Treaty (ratified 1970; extended indefinitely 1995)	Aimed to prevent the spread of nuclear weapons. Recognized the US, UK, France, China and Russia as nuclear weapons states. Nuclear disarmament.	190 signatories, except India, Israel, North Korea, South Sudan and Pakistan. All except South Sudan have successfully acquired nuclear weapons capability.	Little progress on disarmament. States wishing to opt out and develop nuclear weapons have done so.
Treaty of Lisbon (2007)	Amended the European Union constitution. Created new powers for the European Parliament. Created a long-term President of the European Council and a High Representative for Foreign Affairs.	All EU member states. Some member states chose to hold a referendum (France, Netherlands) as part of the ratification process.	Negotiations over the Lisbon Treaty began in 2001. Significant amendments were needed after voters in France and the Netherlands voted against the Treaty in referendums.
Minsk Protocol (2014)	Agreed a ceasefire in Eastern Ukraine with a monitoring mission from the Organization for Security and Cooperation in Europe (OSCE) and a programme of ongoing peace talks.	Ukraine, Russian Federation and two unrecognized state groups representing rebel groups in Eastern Ukraine.	The ceasefire has been broken several times since the Protocol was signed, meaning a new peace agreement was needed just months later.

General vocabulary

treaties formal written agreements between two or more countries or governments

opt out not join a system or accept an agreement

nuclear disarmament the process of getting rid of nuclear weapons

constitution a set of basic laws and principles that a country or organization is governed by

Subject vocabulary

ratified when an individual state's decision to sign an international treaty or convention has been legally approved

Synonyms

amendments . changes

Articulation sentence:

States can cooperate with one another by signing international treaties, however some have been more successful than others.

Strategic alliances

States frequently cooperate more informally, without the need for treaties or international organizations. Choosing reliable and profitable allies and working together on matters of security, trade or development is important if states want to achieve their goals and protect their interests.

Prominent alliances include the so-called 'Special Relationship' between the United States and the United Kingdom. This peaked after the attacks of 11 September 2001 in the US, and the subsequent military campaigns in Afghanistan and Iraq, when the relationship between President George W Bush and Prime Minister Tony Blair became closer, and both states were involved in military action in Iraq and Afghanistan.

Powerful states may decide to form new alliances with less powerful states for **mutual** benefit. For example, China has increased ties with many African states in recent years. China has invested heavily in infrastructure in return for favourable access to the natural resources which China itself lacks. Equally, powerful states may seek closer relations with emerging powers. For example, the United States and China are building economic ties with India and Brazil, both rising economic powers.

> Articulation sentence:
> Some states choose to form informal strategic alliances with others for mutual gain, such as China's investment in Africa in exchange for deals on Africa's natural resources.

General vocabulary

mutual the same for two or more people

1.4 Key concept: Legitimacy

Key idea:

Legitimacy refers to groups or actions that are considered to be acceptable, usually by conforming to agreed laws or democratic principles.

Sources of legitimacy

If groups or actions in global politics are to be considered legitimate, they must be traced back to an agreed source of legitimacy.

Democracy

At a national level, democracy brings legitimacy to governments that wish to exercise control over a particular region. Leaders are democratically elected by popular vote and serve for limited periods. For example, the United States Constitution limits Presidents of the United States to two four-year terms of office. Many states have different ways of electing their leaders. Many do not specify a maximum term for Presidents or Prime Ministers. These rules are legitimately agreed, usually in a constitution.

Political parties seeking elected office must present their proposals for government in a **manifesto**. In the first instance, an elected legislature of representatives checks that they delivered what the manifesto promised. Beyond this, the electorate can choose to reward the government with re-election or choose another at the next election.

Subject vocabulary

manifesto a written statement by a political party, saying what they believe in and what they intend to do if elected

In global politics, democracies are enhanced by:

- the ability of the electorate to participate in elections freely and without intimidation;
- the electorate being able to choose from a wide range of political parties and alternative governments;
- the extent of **checks and balances** on the government. For example, an independent judiciary and an effective legislature.

Balance of power

At a national level, states are often organized so that power is balanced amongst three key branches of government.

Branch	Purpose
Executive	The elected government, which produces policy ideas and implements them.
Legislature	Scrutinizes the proposals of the elected government, votes on whether these proposals should become law and holds the executive to account.
Judiciary	Ensures that the laws proposed by the executive, and agreed by the legislature, are upheld fairly according to the rule of law. The judiciary also ensures that the executive complies with the law and does not exceed its powers.

Constitutions

Many democratic states have a constitution. This clearly sets out and limits the powers of the state, and particularly the branches of government within the state (the executive, judiciary and legislature). Powers that are set out in a constitution are said to be 'fundamental' or 'entrenched', meaning that they are fixed and cannot be changed without going through a lengthy process.

Many states that are rebuilding after conflict go through a process of agreeing a new constitution. The constitution frequently agrees the human rights that citizens of the state will be entitled to. This is central to ensuring that every citizen has an equal stake in society and that the powers of the government are clearly described.

However, some democratic and legitimate states do not have constitutions. The United Kingdom has no written constitution. Instead, its constitutional conventions have been established over time and are contained within many different individual laws.

The rule of law

The rule of law is a key source of legitimacy. This is particularly important for a fair system of justice and human rights. The key principles are that the law is always applied equally to all citizens; that neither citizens nor the government are above the law; and that every citizen has the right to a fair and legitimate trial.

International law

Sovereignty can be confirmed and legitimized in several ways in international law, including through judgements of the International Court of Justice and the UN Security Council.

General vocabulary

checks and balances ways of making sure that someone or something is under control and doing what it should

above the law allowed to not obey the law

Subject vocabulary

judiciary the branch of government that interprets the law and makes judgements on whether individuals and the government are acting lawfully

Beyond this, breaches of customary international law such as the Geneva Conventions would be seen as illegitimate actions, and may result in intervention from other states or groups.

Legitimacy is a key concept relating to peace and conflict. Military action gets its legitimacy from UN Security Council Resolutions that authorize the use of force. For example, UN Security Council Resolution 1973 authorized 'all necessary measures' to protect civilians in Libya in 2011, meaning NATO's military action was widely seen as legitimate. In contrast, the lack of a UN Security Council Resolution directly authorizing the use of force in Iraq in 2003 prompted questions about the legality and legitimacy of the US-led military action.

The following act as other important sources of legitimacy at an international level on matters of international security.

- If a state requests the help of others to defend itself against a threat.
- If a state feels that its national security would be at risk if it did not act, it can invoke Article 51 of the United Nations Charter, which preserves the right of states to individual or collective self-defence. This was used by the United Kingdom as justification for air strikes against Islamic State militants in Syria in 2015.

Articulation sentences:

States and their actions may be considered legitimate in a variety of ways. A state is legitimate if its government is democratically elected, and its actions are legitimate if it adheres to international law.

Legitimacy of non-state groups

NGOs

Non-governmental organizations frequently offer an independent perspective on the legitimacy of government actions. For example, Human Rights Watch and Amnesty International put pressure on governments to improve their codification and protection of human rights laws. NGOs themselves gain legitimacy through both their actions – being seen to be fair and transparent – and through the recognition and status that some IGOs give them, such as the United Nations and the European Union.

IGOs

International organizations gain legitimacy from the treaties and agreements on which they are founded, such as the Treaty of Rome (European Union) and the United Nations Charter (United Nations). IGOs usually have clear procedures and rules stating what their powers and areas of interest are. Some very powerful IGOs, such as the European Union and its European Central Bank, can clash with nation states. In these cases, deciding which side has the greater legitimacy – the elected government of a state or the IGO – can only be done by examining whether the IGO is acting within its powers and whether the state has complied fully with the rules and procedures of the IGO. This tension was seen during the Eurozone crisis. The IMF and the European Central Bank imposed austerity measures on a Eurozone member state, Greece, even though the Greek people had elected an anti-austerity government.

Violent extremist groups

A frequent debate in global politics is whether violent extremist and terrorist groups are fighting a legitimate cause. Often this is summarized as whether 'one person's terrorist is another person's **freedom fighter**'. There is no internationally agreed definition of what terrorism is. Attempts, including by the UN, to agree one have not yet been successful.

There have been many peace negotiations where states have decided not to begin negotiations with groups considered to be acting illegitimately. Confidence-building measures, such as a commitment to non-violence and to peaceful dispute resolution, may give violent extremist groups legitimacy to take part in negotiations (see page vii for 'non-violence' explanation).

Other violent extremist groups may try to justify their violent actions by saying that they have no other option than violent struggle. Where civil and political rights are denied to opposition groups there is a risk that they may **resort to** violence or **civil disobedience**.

Frequently, states and international organizations make public declarations about the illegitimacy and illegality of violent extremist groups. For example, Hamas, the main Islamist movement in Palestine, has been referred to as a terrorist group by the United States, the European Union and many other states. Changing the way they are referred to, in contrast, gives groups greater legitimacy.

Articulation sentence:

NGOs and extremist groups often gain legitimacy through the recognition of states or IGOs, whereas an IGO is usually legitimized by a treaty or formal international agreement.

2.1 Key concept: Human rights

Key idea:

Human rights are the indivisible rights which all human beings are entitled to by virtue of their humanity, without discrimination.

What are human rights?

The United Nations Universal Declaration of Human Rights sets out the global consensus on human rights. It was agreed in 1948. According to the Universal Declaration, human rights follow four key principles. They are universal, interdependent, indivisible and inalienable.

Universal

Universal human rights means that human rights are inherent to human beings and not dependent on other aspects of identity such as nationality, location, age, gender, faith, colour, religion or language. The concept of universality is a key principle in the Universal Declaration of Human Rights and places a duty on all member states, regardless of political, cultural or religious beliefs, to respect fundamental human rights.

Interdependent

Human rights are said to be interdependent because successful protection of one human right helps with the protection of others. Similarly, the denial of one human right will act as a barrier to the effective protection of other human rights. For example, a strong judicial system is likely to universally protect the right to a fair and effective hearing. This then protects other rights, such as freedom from arbitrary detention and arrest. If a government allows arbitrary detention (for example in the case of terrorist suspects) the following rights are at risk:

- Human right to freedom from arbitrary detention;
- Equality before the law (see page vii for 'equality' explanation);
- Right to a fair and effective hearing.

Indivisible

Indivisibility means that all human rights are of equal importance and cannot be arranged into a hierarchy. All human rights must be protected for all human beings. Governments are not permitted to pick and choose some rights over others and may not decide that some rights do not apply to certain individuals or groups. For example, freedom of religion cannot be said to be unimportant and not applied. Human rights in the Universal Declaration come as a full package, to be protected equally.

Inalienable

Closely related to the concept of indivisibility, human rights are considered to be inalienable. This means that they cannot be taken away from (or given away by) human beings, and all human beings are entitled to the full package of rights.

Articulation sentences:

The four features of human rights are that they are universal, interdependent, indivisible and inalienable. They apply to everyone; all of them must be applied; they cannot be placed in a hierarchy and they cannot be removed.

Positive and negative rights

Human rights can also be thought of as either 'positive' or 'negative'.

Negative rights require those in power to step back and let human beings be free from interference. This includes freedom from **torture** and from arbitrary arrest or detention by the state. All of these rights are protected through the inaction of those in power. Protecting negative rights should be feasible regardless of financial constraints, though they may be particularly at risk when governments feel they face a security threat.

Positive rights require positive action by those in power. For example, the right to free education cannot be protected without the government actively providing adequate schools, teachers, classrooms and materials. The same positive action from government is needed to provide an adequate judicial system, which allows individuals to enjoy the human right to a fair and effective public hearing by a tribunal. Without government intervention these rights would be not be delivered and would be meaningless. Protecting positive rights is therefore more challenging for governments in less economically developed countries, though the concept of 'progressive realization' recognizes that not all governments or states will be able to provide such interventions as quickly.

Articulation sentence:

Positive human rights are those in which the government must take action to protect the people; negative rights require the government not to act to allow certain freedoms.

2.2 Key concept: Justice

Key idea:

Justice is the concept of fair treatment, usually based on an agreed and accepted set of laws that are applied equally, universally and with the right to a fair trial.

Human rights, when properly codified and protected, are an essential part of an effective and fair justice system. Although there is no fixed definition, justice implies fairness and equality of treatment delivered through a concept known as the rule of law. One of the earliest interpretations comes from Aristotle, who said that 'it is better for the law to rule than one of the citizens, so even the guardians of the laws are obeying the laws'.

The rule of law is commonly agreed to comprise the following principles, which make up the central features of an effective and fair justice system:

- **No one is above the law**, especially those in positions of power. Presidents, prime ministers and governments must all comply with the law, including human rights laws. According to the concept of the rule of law, it is literally the law that rules supreme.

- **The right to a fair trial**. The law must be applied and interpreted fairly by independent courts and judges. The law should not be enforced arbitrarily by governments. Those accused of offences should have the right to defend themselves in a court of law.

- **All are subject to the same law**, applied to all citizens equally. The law is not applied inconsistently, with some allowed to escape justice and others not. The law must be consistent in its content; new laws cannot be invented arbitrarily.

Subject vocabulary

negative rights rights that require individuals to be left alone and not interfered with by the government or other powers (e.g. freedom from torture)

security threat a threat to the peace and safety of a state or group of people

positive rights rights that require the government to take action and to provide services (e.g. health or education) that allow certain rights to be enjoyed by individuals

tribunal a legally established panel with judicial powers to settle a criminal case or other dispute

codified written down in a legal form and agreed upon by a state or international organisation

rule of law the concept that no one, including the government, is above the law and that a state is ultimately ruled only by what is lawful

General vocabulary

torture the deliberate use of extreme physical violence to force someone to say or do something against their wishes

intervention the act of becoming involved in an argument, conflict or other difficult situation in order to change what happens

above the law allowed to not obey the law

Synonyms

feasible .... possible

General vocabulary

intimidating frightening or threatening someone into making them do what you want

progressively happening or developing gradually over a period of time

degrading treatment an unpleasant experience or event that makes you lose respect for yourself

Subject vocabulary

civil rights rights that belong to a citizen by virtue of being a citizen of a particular country, including protection from racial discrimination

political rights rights that allow citizens to participate in politics, for example by voting and having the freedom to demonstrate and join political parties

For human rights to be properly **upheld**, the government or those in power must be subject to the rule of law. This is a particularly important principle, since governments are the most dangerous potential violators of human rights. This is because those in power also have the possibility of evading investigation and prosecution, perhaps by **intimidating** judges or simply ignoring and blocking effective protection of human rights.

Articulation sentence:
> An effective justice system must be governed by the rule of law and not by those in power, meaning that: everyone is subject to the same law; no one is above the law; everyone has the right to a fair trial.

2.3 Key concept: Liberty

Key idea:

Liberty is about the freedom of individuals to live a life without excessive interference from those in power, and with the freedom to flourish and make the most of opportunities.

Human rights have developed **progressively** over many centuries, existing in some form as early as the Magna Carta in 13th-century England. In the 17th century, European philosophers including John Locke, Hugo Grotius and Jean-Jacques Rousseau attempted to define the relationship, or social contract, between individuals and the authority of the state.

Despite these discussions many centuries earlier, the first expression of human rights as a global framework agreed by nation states for nation states to follow came with the foundation of the United Nations. The UN agreed the Universal Declaration of Human Rights in 1948.

First-generation rights focus on the **civil** and **political rights** that protect individuals' **liberty** from the state (see page vi for 'liberty' explanation). They are **predominantly** negative rights, where the state steps back from the private sphere of an individual's life and allows the individual to enjoy basic rights such as the right to life, liberty and property. Such rights are also called natural rights, meaning that they are central to what it means to be a human and therefore are inalienable and cannot be taken away.

Articles 3 to 21 of the Universal Declaration and the 1966 International Covenant on Civil and Political Rights are the **core** first-generation, or civil and political, rights. They include the rights to:

- life, liberty and property
- freedom from torture, and cruel and **degrading treatment**
- freedom of thought, conscience and religion
- equality for everyone before the law
- freedom from arbitrary arrest and detention.

Articulation sentences:
> First-generation human rights cover civil and political rights, such as the right to life, freedom of thought and religion, and freedom from arbitrary arrest. They are mostly negative rights.

2.4 Key concept: Equality

Key idea:

Equality is the idea that people are treated the same, without discrimination, and are allowed to enjoy the same opportunities.

Second-generation rights focus on the economic, social and cultural rights that allow citizens to flourish within the state. They are predominantly positive rights. This means the state actively provides public services in order to deliver rights to which every human being is entitled. This generation of rights is aimed at delivering equality of opportunity for each citizen.

Articles 22 to 27 of the Universal Declaration and the 1966 International Covenant on Economic, Social and Cultural Rights set out the core second-generation, or economic, social and cultural, rights. They include the rights to:

- free education up to secondary level
- work and to equal pay for equal work
- a standard of living adequate to the health and well-being of the individual and his or her family (including food, healthcare, clothing, housing and social services)
- adequate rest and leisure.

Clearly, less economically developed countries may protest that it is not possible to guarantee second-generation rights due to limited resources, both human and financial. The United Nations takes this into account, and places an obligation of progressive realization upon states. This means that the United Nations recognizes that realization of these rights 'can be hampered by a lack of resources and can be achieved only over a period of time'. Consequently, states' compliance with second-generation rights takes into account the resources available and the progress that states are making towards full protection of the rights.

Articulation sentence:

Second-generation human rights are mostly positive and require governments to provide free education, adequate healthcare and to protect the right of equal pay.

Third-generation rights are less clearly defined than the previous two generations. They are broadly seen to apply primarily to communities at global, international, regional, national and local levels, rather than to individuals. They focus on protection of the environment, on peace and on development, making each a matter of collective human rights, as well as a policy goal to be achieved in its own right. Frequently, they attempt to codify the rights and responsibilities that states and communities have in protecting the environment that they share. Key documents said to express third-generation rights are the 1972 Stockholm Declaration on the Human Environment and the Declaration at the 1992 UN Earth Summit in Rio de Janeiro, which agreed that:

- human beings are entitled to a healthy life in harmony with nature;
- the right to development must be fulfilled so as to equitably meet developmental and environmental needs of present and future generations (sustainable development);
- peace, development and environmental protection are interdependent and indivisible.

General vocabulary

flourish develop well and be successful

adequate enough in quantity or of a good enough quality for a particular purpose

obligation a formal, legally stated requirement to do something

realization the process of achieving something

Subject vocabulary

public services the services, such as education and healthcare, which a government might chose to provide collectively for people in a state

economic rights rights that enable individuals to enjoy economic prosperity and freedom

social rights rights that enable citizens to enjoy access to basic social services such as health and education

cultural rights rights that enable citizens to have their culture and identity recognized and celebrated

collective human rights rights held by groups on the basis of identified group characteristics

Synonyms

hampered ..... made difficult

first-generation rights	second-generation rights	third-generation rights
Political and civil rights	Economic and social rights	Cultural and collective rights
Predominantly negative rights	Predominantly positive rights	

Figure 2.1 *Development of human rights timeline*

Articulation sentence:
Third-generation human rights are aimed at protecting the environment; peace and development are therefore seen as collective rights.

Violations of human rights

The primary responsibility for upholding and protecting human rights lies with those in power, and with nation states in particular. If power is spread beyond nation-state level, other groups – for example, rebel forces in a civil war or leaders of ethnic or tribal groups – also have a responsibility to uphold and protect human rights. Abuses of human rights are usually systemic. This means that abuses are committed against numerous victims within a society, or that abuses have become part of the society's system of government and how the society operates.

Examples of human rights abuses include:

Abuse	Human rights violated
Human trafficking	The right to freedom of movement; to life; to liberty and security; to not be subject to torture or cruel and degrading treatment; to just and favourable conditions of work.
Use of child soldiers	The right to life, survival and development; protection of best interests of the child; protection from all forms of violence, abuse, neglect and ill treatment. (These rights are underpinned by the UN Convention on the Rights of the Child, agreed in 1989, which set out the specific duties owed to children to ensure that all children can enjoy all their rights.)
Female genital mutilation (FGM)	The right to life; to not be subject to torture or cruel or degrading treatment; protection from all forms of violence and abuse; full and equal participation of women in political, civil, economic, social and cultural life; the eradication of all forms of discrimination on the grounds of gender.

Articulation sentences:
Leaders of tribal groups and rebel forces also have a duty to uphold human rights. Some examples of violation of these rights include human trafficking, the use of child soldiers, and female genital mutilation.

Relationships between the generations

The three generations of human rights provide a useful means of tracking how human rights have developed internationally since 1948. At first sight, there is a clear division between the largely negative civil and political rights and the positive economic, social and cultural rights that followed. However, the relationships between the generations should not be overlooked, given the important principle of interdependence that the Universal Declaration emphasizes. There is strong evidence of this interdependence. For example, a lack of education, employment or fair pay (second-generation, economic, social and cultural rights) is likely to impede an individual from fully exercising his or her political freedoms (first-generation, political and civil rights). Similarly, disease or hunger is less likely to occur where all individuals have an equal political voice and a stake in society and are able to challenge injustice.

There are relationships too between the third-generation of collective human rights and first- and second-generation rights. Peace and development (third-generation, collective rights) are less likely to flourish in states that offer no political empowerment or means of dispute resolution (first-generation, civil and political rights). Clashes over resources may be resolved violently rather than peacefully, leading to poverty and instability.

> **Articulation sentence:**
> First-, second- and third-generation human rights are interconnected and where some rights are lacking this may prevent other rights being fulfilled.

Key human rights laws

Since the end of the Second World War, new human rights laws and conventions have been created at international, regional and national levels. Human rights laws have developed both in content (see the generations of human rights) and jurisdiction. Key documents (and their strengths and weaknesses) include the following.

Signed / created	Human rights law	Strengths	Weaknesses
1948	Universal Declaration of Human Rights	First international consensus on universal human rights. An aspirational document that has influenced binding international covenants, regional conventions and the human rights laws of nation states.	Non-binding in international law. Critics of a universal approach say that it imposes a Western or Judeo-Christian viewpoint of human rights.
1950	European Convention on Human Rights	The first regional agreement on human rights. A binding legal text, which member states are committed to act in accordance with. The European Court of Human Rights acts as a final court of appeal of last resort once European citizens have exhausted their own state's legal process.	Decisions of the European Court are binding, but there is still no means of enforcement, as nation states can still ignore decisions of the Court if they chose to. Sovereignty may come under pressure if the European Court of Human Rights judges disagree with national governments and legislatures.

Synonyms

impede .... prevent

General vocabulary

stake in if you have a stake in something, you will get advantages if it is successful, and you feel that you have an important connection with it

instability when a situation is not certain because there is the possibility of sudden change

binding a promise or agreement that must be obeyed

Subject vocabulary

injustice a situation in which people are treated unfairly and not given their rights

empowerment the ability for citizens of a state to be involved in decision-making

dispute resolution mechanisms and systems for resolving disagreements

European Court of Human Rights regional court which upholds the European Convention on Human Rights, established in 1959

sovereignty the power that an independent country has to govern itself

Signed / created	Human rights law	Strengths	Weaknesses
1966	International Covenants on Economic and Social Rights; and Civil and Political Rights	First legally binding international human rights laws. Clarified rights set out in the Universal Declaration. Prohibition of slavery and torture is one of several Articles set out in much greater detail.	Economic and social rights are more difficult for less developed nations to deliver, although it is accepted that such rights may be realized progressively. No international enforcement body. States cannot be forced to uphold these rights. Civil and political rights in particular are still violated worldwide.
1984	Convention against Torture and Other Cruel, Inhuman and Degrading Treatment	Builds on the Universal Declaration and the International Covenant on Civil and Political Rights. Offers specific definitions of torture and the responsibilities for preventing torture. Prohibits nation states from relying on evidence gained through torture by other nation states. Includes the duty to protect all human beings (not just a state's own citizens) from torture.	The Convention cannot be enforced and states that have signed and ratified the Convention can still carry out torture. For example, President Obama confirmed in 2015 that 'in the immediate aftermath of 9/11, we did some things that were wrong. We did a whole lot of things that were right, but we tortured some folks. We did things that were contrary to our values.'
1986	African Charter on Human and People's Rights	The Charter has provided a process for African Union states to agree on new human rights. For example, a Protocol on Women's Rights in 2003 addressed issues relating to FGM. Recognizes collective rights, as well as individual rights.	Difficult to enforce decisions of the African Commission on Human Rights on member states, because the Commission does not have any formal enforcement powers and its recommendations are not legally binding on member states.

Signed / created	Human rights law	Strengths	Weaknesses
1997	**Constitution of South Africa**	One example of human rights protection at nation-state level (many more exist). The Bill of Rights, enshrined into Chapter 2 of the South African Constitution, mirrors closely the Universal Declaration of Human Rights. Most of these rights were denied during South Africa's apartheid rule which divided the white and black communities.	The Bill of Rights allows for judges to interpret certain rights as having limits, rather than being absolute.
1998	**Rome Statute**	Creates an international court for hearing cases relating to breaches of international criminal law, including crimes against humanity. Powers to issue arrest warrants. Powers to launch special investigations into alleged breaches of international criminal law. Countries that have not signed the Rome Statute can be investigated if the UN Security Council agrees to it.	Not all member states have signed and ratified the Rome Statute. These states cannot be held accountable to the International Criminal Court. In particular, three of the permanent members of the UN Security Council (China, Russia and the US) have not ratified the Rome Statute. As of 2015, only two breaches of international criminal law have resulted in convictions. Both related to African conflicts, prompting accusations from the African Union that the ICC is biased against Africa. In 2014, the African Union member states narrowly voted against withdrawing from the Rome Statute.

Upholding human rights

Ensuring that individuals' human rights are upheld depends on the relationship between four core responsibilities carried out by international organizations, states, civil society and others.

Codification	Human rights need to be formalized in law. This can be done at international level (for example, the International Covenant on Civil and Political Rights); at regional level (for example, the European Convention on Human Rights); or at national level (for example, the UK Human Rights Act 1998). Codification is no guarantee of effective protection, but can provide a legal basis for protection to take place.
Protection	Once set out in law, human rights need to be actively protected. The most effective way is for independent courts to adjudicate on breaches of human rights law. National courts are usually the only option for judicial protection, except in the case of the European Court of Human Rights which acts as a court of appeal for cases in member states of the Council of Europe.
Promotion	Human rights need to be actively promoted both before and after they have been effectively codified. This involves a wide range of groups from governments, international organizations and civil society championing specific human rights. Nation states may promote human rights and encourage other states to follow their example through a positive track record of codification and enforcement. NGOs such as Human Rights Watch and Amnesty are high-profile promoters of human rights, frequently highlighting gaps in codification and protection. For example, the United States has advanced gay rights within their country and is now seeking to promote the same rights in Africa.
Monitoring	Human rights need to be actively monitored by independent bodies to ensure that governments are complying with their own national laws, commitments they have made in international law, and international norms and standards more generally. The UN Human Rights Council and the UN High Commissioner for Human Rights, along with human rights NGOs, are the principal actors in this area.

❝ Articulation sentence:
Human rights must be codified in law, protected by courts, promoted by governments and key groups, and monitored by independent bodies.

General vocabulary

adjudicate officially decide who is right in a disagreement and decide what should be done

bodies a group of people who work together to do a particular job or who are together for a particular purpose

Subject vocabulary

Council of Europe regional organisation of 47 European states, established in 1949 (not to be confused with the European Union)

NGOs non-government organizations

UN Human Rights Council part of the United Nations responsible for monitoring and upholding international human rights, established in 2006

UN High Commissioner for Human Rights appointed official of the United Nations who leads efforts to uphold international human rights

Challenges in upholding human rights

All four of these responsibilities present major challenges.

<table>
<tr>
<td>

Codification

</td>
<td>

International

The Universal Declaration of Human Rights (1948) is a statement of guiding principles. It has had a powerful influence on global human rights, but was not binding for member states. The International Covenants of 1966 on Economic, Social and Cultural Rights, and Civil and Political Rights were introduced to formally codify the Universal Declaration into international law. However, unlike national laws – which have national courts to enforce them – there is no international court to enforce the rights that states have signed up to. Member states may also simply not sign up to or ratify international treaties and laws governing human rights. For example, in 2015, Saudi Arabia came under international pressure to ratify the International Covenant on Civil and Political Rights. Furthermore, three members of the UN Security Council (China, Russia and the US) have either not ratified or signed the 1998 Rome Statute that created the International Criminal Court.

Regional

Regional attempts at codification can be prone to modification. The European Convention of Human Rights is a powerful, binding law that closely follows the Universal Declaration. It is a useful safeguard and is the basis for a court of appeal for European member states. Clashes between nation states and the European Court do occur on matters of interpretation, with nation states complaining that their sovereignty is challenged by regional interpretations of human rights law.

Sometimes, states omit or modify human rights set out in the Universal Declaration because of cultural relativism. For example, the Cairo Declaration on Human Rights in Islam neglects freedom of religion. The African Charter of Human Rights emphasizes human rights as collective, rather than individual.

National

Potentially, national codification is the most powerful means of codification. This is because nation states often possess national courts which can actually adjudicate and take action in cases where human rights are abused. However, national human rights laws may be prone to cultural relativism and selective interpretation, may be modified in response to events, or may not exist at all.

</td>
</tr>
</table>

Synonyms

prone .... likely

modification .. change

Subject vocabulary

relativism the argument that rights should be modified to take account of differences between states and cultures

> ❝ **Articulation sentence:**
> Codification of human rights is more effective at the national level than the international or regional level where there are fewer courts to enforce the law.

court of last resort the court
in which a final appeal against a
decision of a lower court may be
made

Protection

International

The international community lacks any meaningful protection body. The exceptions are rare cases of international criminal law for the most serious crimes against humanity. The International Criminal Court or international criminal tribunals have jurisdiction over such cases (for example, after the Rwanda **genocide** and the civil wars in the former Yugoslavia). The International Criminal Court is criticized for its low level of convictions. In over 30 cases brought to the court, so far only three have been convicted.

Regional

The European Court of Human Rights has the power to make binding decisions on nation states. Such decisions are frequently disputed or ignored by nation states, which complain that national sovereignty is being challenged. For example, the United Kingdom resisted a European Court judgement requiring prisoners to be given the vote. Regional courts for the Americas and Africa (created in 1979 and 2004 respectively) are a **court of last resort**, with greater emphasis placed on resolving matters diplomatically through regional human rights commissions, perhaps recognizing tensions with national sovereignty.

National

The key dilemma at the national level is that the state is both the most likely violator of human rights and has the principal responsibility for protecting and enforcing human rights. Nation states may therefore choose to ignore human rights abuses that it is itself carrying out (for example, human rights abuses in Syria under President Bashar al-Assad).

Articulation sentences:
Protection of human rights at the international and regional level is challenged by the inability of courts to enforce the law on member states. National courts cannot always be depended on to protect human rights because they are often the violators of those rights.

Promotion

International

International organizations such as the United Nations and its associated bodies, the UN Human Rights Council and the UN High Commissioner for Human Rights, can be powerful **advocates** for human rights. However, the UN Human Rights Council is often criticized for defending the interests of its member states, some of which themselves have questionable human rights records.

International human rights NGOs are very powerful promoters of human rights. They produce regular rights-specific reports on, for example, **LGBT**, and **lobby** both national governments and international organizations to take action. However, their power to publicize human rights issues (much enhanced by social media and the internet) is not always matched by their power to change the behaviour of human rights abusers.

Regional

The African Commission for Human Rights is much more heavily used than its Court for Human Rights. It has played a successful role in promoting better treatment of prisoners. However, the Commission is prone to selective investigation and has done little to promote LGBT rights, which are denied by many African states.

National

Effective national promotion of human rights suffers the same constraints as protection. In other words, states that grossly abuse human rights are the most likely to prevent public debate about or challenges to their human rights record. For example, under Saddam Hussein, Iraq severely restricted public gatherings and **dissent**.

> **Articulation sentence:**
> The promotion of human rights suffers in nations who do not uphold them, and at regional and international levels where it is not always unbiased.

General vocabulary

advocates people who publicly support someone or something

dissent refusal to agree with an official decision or accepted opinion

Subject vocabulary

LGBT lesbian, gay, bisexual and transgender people

lobby try to persuade the government or someone with political power that a law or situation should be changed

International

The UN Human Rights Council and the UN High Commissioner for Human Rights have the power to conduct in-depth reviews of both individual states' human rights records and the global protection of specific human rights. The effectiveness of such monitoring depends on the receptiveness of the nation state to any criticism.

Regional

The African Human Rights Commission places great emphasis on monitoring African states' human rights arrangements. Similarly, the Inter-American Commission on Human Rights has a primary role in monitoring its member states' protection of human rights. Frequently, however, member states that abuse human rights may be unstable or in conflict, making it unsafe to conduct thorough investigations. Human rights NGOs, such as Amnesty and Human Rights Watch, are often able to expose abuses because they source evidence from local civil society activists. Such evidence is frequently filmed using cheap mobile phones and is broadcast on the internet.

National

States with well-developed human rights arrangements often create and enshrine in law a specific monitoring agency at national level. For example, the UK's Equality and Human Rights Commission is a high-profile and independent voice that challenges the UK government's human rights record. Once again, the most likely abusers of human rights are unlikely to create or empower such bodies and responsibility for monitoring will be left to civil society activists or NGOs.

Articulation sentence:
The role of monitoring often falls to objective NGOs or other organizations, particularly in states abusing human rights who are unwilling to monitor their own record.

Human rights and power

Human rights are inextricably linked with power dynamics that exist in global politics. These can be seen most obviously at national and international level.

At the national level, it is clear that the nation state has considerable power over the effective or ineffective protection of human rights within its territory. States with *too much* internal power and states with *too little* internal power are both likely to be poor protectors of human rights.

A state with too little internal power will have weak internal sovereignty, such as fragile states like Somalia and Libya. Here, the central government may have lost political control of large parts of its territory and will therefore probably not be able to uphold human rights effectively. The state's judicial system – its courts and judges – is likely to be in disarray. States or regions in conflict find little opportunity to uphold human rights amid the instability of conflict.

A state with too much internal power will have a dominant central authority which may decide either to actively abuse or suspend human rights for its own political purposes. For example, the Syrian government's use of chemical weapons in 2014 against its own citizens is a conscious abuse of human rights. Equally, a powerful state may decide to suspend human rights for some of its citizens. The United States was criticized for its use of torture against terrorist suspects in the aftermath of the 11 September 2001 terrorist attacks and for holding suspects without charge at Guantanamo Bay in Cuba (outside the official national jurisdiction of the United States). Even states that helped to develop the foundational documents of international human rights law can sometimes fail in their responsibility to protect human rights.

At the national level, the best chance for effective protection of human rights is when power is *in balance*. Crucially, this involves a separation of powers between the government (executive), parliament (legislature) and the courts (judiciary). Problems arise in particular when the executive branch of government becomes either too weak or too powerful.

> ❝ Articulation sentence:
>
> For human rights to be protected effectively a nation's power must be in balance between the government, the parliament and the courts.

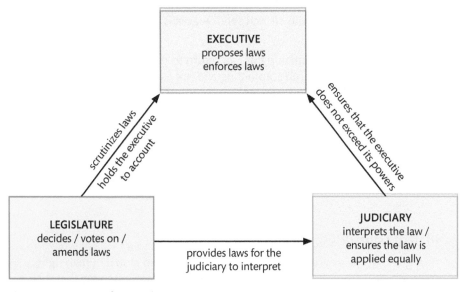

Figure 2.2 *Separation of powers diagram*

The unique role played by nation states in protecting human rights is summarized in the dilemma that the nation state is the most likely or principal violator of human rights, whilst being the essential protector of human rights.

If nation states fail to protect human rights, the international community may be expected to step in. There are several ways it can do this.

Responsible sovereignty is the notion, endorsed by the UN General Assembly in 2004, that nation states forfeit their sovereignty if they fail in their duty to protect their citizens. If a state fails to exercise responsible sovereignty, other nation states have a responsibility to protect. They may call upon the UN Security Council to authorize military intervention or non-military actions, such as sanctions.

For example, when Muammar Gaddafi threatened to kill civilians who opposed him in the Arab Uprisings in 2011, the UN Security Council agreed to intervene and launched air strikes to stop the advance of government forces. The UN Security Council did not agree to respond with military force to President Bashar al-Assad's use of chemical weapons in Syria in 2013. However, it did agree to a non-military solution to disarm the Syrian government of its chemical weapons.

However, the international community could be criticized for failing to agree on intervention when nation states are committing human rights abuses. For example:

- There was no international intervention to prevent genocide in Darfur, Sudan in 2004, despite the widespread international condemnation for failing to prevent genocide in Rwanda a decade earlier.
- In the Syrian civil war, non-military action was approved by the UN Security Council to deal with chemical weapons. However, widespread human rights abuses committed by government and rebel forces before and since have not been challenged and continue without impunity.

Pressure may be exerted in the form of sanctions and trade bans, such as those imposed on Myanmar for the military government's imprisonment of pro-democracy leader Aung San Suu Kyi. But sanctions such as this do not produce quick results. Sanctions may not have much effect on those in power – unlike the wider population – and so nation states may decide to resist the pressure.

Frequently, governments are accused of not putting enough pressure on economically powerful nation states with questionable human rights records:

- China's economic power means that many governments pursue friendly trade relations with China, at the expense of challenging China's human rights record.
- The West's relationship with oil-rich Saudi Arabia is frequently the source of similar accusations.

Discussions of power and human rights can return to the dilemma that nation states remain hugely powerful in both committing and preventing human rights abuses. As long as nation states retain sovereignty and control of their own affairs in global politics, the options open to the international community will remain limited.

> **Articulation sentence:**
> When a nation does not protect its citizens' human rights, other nations can request the UN Security Council to take military or non-military action to prevent the abuse of rights.

Cultural relativism

Some argue that the desire for a single set of universal and global human rights clashes with cultural, ethnic or religious values. Nation states often say that their unique cultural or religious identities are not compatible with the rights set out in the Universal Declaration of Human Rights. This notion of cultural relativism challenges universalism by suggesting that human rights are defined by the immediate local culture and values, rather than by a global set of universal values. Critics of relativism argue that these states are guilty of picking and choosing their human rights to suit political circumstances, or failing to challenge outdated cultural, ethnic or religious values.

Relativism may be driven both by government policies and at community level (as in the example of community practice of female genital mutilation). Frequently, government policy and community traditions reinforce each other. For example, governments may not challenge cultural practices sufficiently through effective investigation, prosecution and conviction, allowing these cultural practices to continue.

General vocabulary

impunity freedom from fear of prosecution or punishment

Subject vocabulary

cultural relativism the theory that ideas and other norms should reflect cultural practices and traditions, rather than universal principles

universalism the idea that rights should be equally applicable to all people or countries, and do not vary according to local cultures or religious beliefs

values widely accepted ideas about what is right and wrong, or what is important in life

Example	Claim: Cultural relativism is justified	Counterclaim: Cultural relativism is not justified
Women's rights – Saudi Arabia Saudi Arabia has a male guardianship system where women are subject to different rights to men. Women are not permitted to obtain a passport, marry, travel or access higher education without the approval of a male guardian. Women are banned from driving and are not allowed to expose parts of their bodies except in a medical emergency.	Responding to a UN Human Rights Council report in 2013, the Saudi government said that the Kingdom of Saudi Arabia is governed by Sharia law, under which Muslim rulers have to promote and protect human rights, as prescribed in the Holy Qur'an. They argued, 'Sharia law guarantees equality of the sexes on the basis of the principle of the **complementarity** of rights and duties.' In spite of the male guardianship system, the Saudi government claimed that the number of women enrolled in higher education exceeds the number of men. The Saudi government also confirmed that the ruling Shura Council had been amended to ensure that women occupy 20 per cent of the seats. 30 women joined the Council in 2013.	Amnesty International reported that women have subordinate status to men under the law and remain subject to discrimination, 'particularly in relation to family matters such as marriage, divorce, child custody and inheritance'. Women and girls remained 'inadequately protected against sexual and other violence', with domestic violence **'endemic'** despite efforts by the government to raise awareness of the problem. A 2013 law criminalizing domestic violence was 'not implemented due to a lack of competent authorities to enforce it'. Prominent women's rights activists had been detained, some under 'terrorism-related' charges.

General vocabulary

complementarity a relationship where two or more different things improve each other's qualities

endemic a problem which is always present in a particular place, or among a particular group of people

Example	Claim: Cultural relativism is justified	Counterclaim: Cultural relativism is not justified
Female genital mutilation – Egypt Despite being illegal since 2008, the UN estimates that Egypt has the highest rate of FGM in the world. In 2014, Egyptian government figures estimated that as many as 90 per cent of women under 50 have experienced it. Most victims of FGM are aged between 7 and 10 years old.	Female genital mutilation is particularly prevalent in Africa and some Middle Eastern countries. It is not linked to any single religion and occurs in both Christian and Muslim societies. Justification is therefore cultural, not religious. It is used to control women's sexuality and fertility by mutilating their sex organs to ensure chastity.	In 2007, Egypt's Grand Mufti issued a statement saying that 'the harmful tradition of circumcision that is practised in Egypt in our era is forbidden' in Islam. In 2014, Human Rights Watch criticized the lack of effective enforcement of laws protecting girls from FGM, following the initial acquittal of a doctor accused of carrying out the procedure in Egypt's first FGM trial. Human Rights Watch said, 'FGM is banned in Egypt but the practice continues possibly because there is a lack of investigations, prosecutions and convictions.' In January 2015, the doctor was convicted of the manslaughter of a 13-year-old girl.
LGBT rights – Uganda Uganda's parliament passed an Anti-Homosexuality Act in 2013, increasing prison sentences for same-sex conduct and criminalizing the 'promotion of homosexuality'. The law was deemed unconstitutional by Uganda's Supreme Court in 2015. However, the Court challenged the procedures behind the parliamentary vote, rather than the content of the law. The government responded by proposing new legislation.	Uganda's President, Yoweri Museveni, defended the law in 2015, telling CNN, 'I am acting on behalf of the society. I would like to advise the Europeans and Western groups that this should be a no-go area. This is one area they are not going to make our people budge. We cannot accept that living unnaturally is a human right.'	Human Rights Watch reported in 2014, that 'with the passage of the Anti-Homosexuality Act, some LGBT people reported increased arbitrary arrests, police abuse and extortion, loss of employment, and evictions.' President Obama, visiting Kenya and Uganda in 2015, said, 'I believe in the principle of treating people equally under the law, and that they are deserving of equal protection under the law and that the state should not discriminate against people based on their sexual orientation. And I say that, recognizing that

Example	Claim: Cultural relativism is justified	Counterclaim: Cultural relativism is not justified
		there may be people who have different religious or cultural beliefs. The state does not need to give an opinion on religious doctrine. The state just has to say we're going to treat everybody equally under the law.'

 Articulation sentence:
Cultural relativism states that values are defined by local culture as opposed to global ideology, however it has been criticized as a means for nations to pick and choose which rights they are willing to uphold.

Politicization of human rights

There is a general lack of consistency regarding which states are challenged about their human rights records by other states and by the United Nations. This lack of consistency is a further challenge when it comes to protecting human rights globally.

The UN Human Rights Council has faced particular criticism. Critics accuse the Council of a disproportionate focus on Israel at the expense of other human rights violations. Furthermore, the membership of the Human Rights Council includes many member states whose own human rights records are questionable. Critics say this makes the Council an ineffective protector of global human rights, with member states reluctant to condemn other states for human rights abuses of which they themselves are also guilty.

In 2013, the African Union claimed that the decisions of the International Criminal Court were biased against African states. As of 2015, the only successful convictions have been of Africans (Thomas Lubanga, Germain Katanga and Jean-Pierre Bemba, for crimes committed in the Democratic Republic of Congo). The majority of cases investigated and arrest warrants issued are in relation to African states.

The UN Security Council has the power to authorize military action in states which fail to protect human rights and exercise sovereignty responsibly. Critics see politicization here too, with a failure to compel Israel to comply with UN Security Council resolutions. Whereas other states – notably Iraq, under Saddam Hussein – are the target of sanctions, weapons inspections and other Security Council-approved measures, in order to force them to comply with UN Security Council resolutions.

Articulation sentence:
A major challenge to human rights protection is the lack of consistency in treatment of rights violations in different states, caused by political issues.

CHALLENGE YOURSELF

Thinking, Communication and Social skills

Do you think cultural relativism is justified? Discuss your thoughts in groups then write a table with arguments for and against.

3.1 Key concept: Development

Key idea:

Most simply, development means a **sustained** increase in the standard of living in a society.

What is development?

The exact definition of development is debated

Development is often measured by economic growth. There is no doubt that a well-managed economy is necessary for an increased standard of living. However, many would argue that development involves more than just economic growth. Critics of the purely economic view argue that social and political factors, such as human rights and democracy, are equally important in development.

People often refer to Maslow's **hierarchy** of needs in the context of development. It shows a progression from basic human needs such as food and **shelter** at the bottom of the hierarchy, to higher needs such relationships and self-esteem further up the hierarchy. The goal is **self-actualization**, or the fulfillment of a person's potential and wishes in life. The pyramid structure shows that if the bottom levels are not secure, it will be difficult to achieve the upper levels. Development can thus be defined as the struggle to fulfill human needs, from basic biological needs to higher goals.

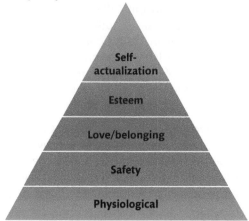

Fig 3.1 *Maslow's hierarchy of needs*

However, other **scholars** have criticized this hierarchical outlook on development. They argue that for a **dignified** life, all basic needs are equally important.

Human development

Human development refers to the process of enlarging people's freedoms and opportunities, and improving their well-being (Haq, 1990). It is more individual focused than socio-political development. Human development focuses on the freedom of ordinary people and how this impacts who they want to be and how they want to live their lives. There is a focus on **capabilities** which refers to the necessary equipment people have to pursue a life of value. Examples of basic capabilities include good health, access to knowledge, the level of control over living environment and freedom from violence.

Economic development

Economic development refers to economic growth. The aim of economic development is to increase productivity and revenue, to establish new industries and innovate, and to diversify the economy into many different sectors, rather than relying on one main resource for trade.

Socio-political development

Socio-political development refers to social developments, for example **gender equality** and education levels. Scholars also emphasize the political aspects of development, such as democratic and responsible governments, low **corruption** levels, and an independent and impartial legal system.

Development as freedom

Development as freedom refers to people's access to choice. The economist Amartya Sen argues that development is a way to increase people's ability to live a free, fulfilled and happy life. He emphasizes the goals of development, rather than the methods. He observes that a lot of academic debates revolve around details of policies and their implementation, and lose sight of the overall aim of development. Economic growth does not automatically lead to development. Notions of freedom must be included in the debate.

Articulation sentence:
> Scholars disagree on the correct definition of development, as it can be defined in economic, social, political or other terms.

How is development measured?

Income-based measures of development

The simplest **measures** of development are income-based. Examples of income-based measures are GDP per capita, as well as the Gini coefficient. To calculate GDP per capita, the overall income of a country is divided by the number of its inhabitants. This gives us the average income per person, or what each person would earn if everybody earned exactly the same salary. When GDP per capita is increasing, this means that the economy is growing, and it is an indicator of development. If there is no growth, or a downward trend, this means that there is negative development. A major advantage of this measure is that it is simple – data on national GDP and the number of inhabitants is easy to get for most countries. A weakness is that GDP per capita does not consider how the income in a country is distributed, as it looks only at the average. In very unequal societies, GDP per capita can be a misleading measure – if the rich are getting richer, this may show in an increase in GDP per capita, even though the situation of the poor did not change at all.

The Gini coefficient is used to measure how equal or unequal societies are. It considers the distribution of income, rather than assuming that it is distributed evenly. It measures the difference between the incomes of the richest and of the poorest, and how many people earn how much on this spectrum. The Gini coefficient is given as a number between 0 and 1. The more equal a society is, the closer to 0 its Gini coefficient. A high Gini coefficient indicates that there is a lot of inequality in society and great difference between the incomes of the wealthiest and the poorest (see page vii for 'inequality' explanation). The Gini coefficient can be used as an indicator for development, assuming that high inequality is bad for development. It is used to **complement** the overall picture provided by GDP per capita.

(see page vii for 'inequality' explanation)

Synonyms

revenue .... income

impartial .... unbiased

indicator .... sign

distributed .... shared

spectrum .... range

General vocabulary

innovate start to use new ideas, methods or inventions

diversify change something or make it change so that there is more variety

gender equality a situation in which men and women have the same rights and advantages

corruption dishonest, illegal or immoral behaviour, especially from someone with power

measures ways of assessing something

complement make a good combination with someone or something else

Subject vocabulary

GDP per capita the total value of all goods and services produced in a country, in one year, except for income received from abroad; divided by the number of people in a country

Gini coefficient a statistical method of modelling and graphing the extent of wealth inequality in a society

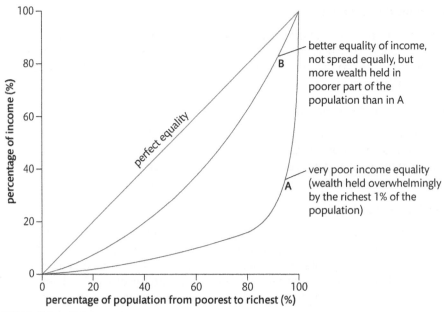

Fig 3.2 *Gini coefficient*

On the chart:
- better equality of income, not spread equally, but more wealth held in poorer part of the population than in A (label B)
- very poor income equality (wealth held overwhelmingly by the richest 1% of the population) (label A)
- perfect equality

y-axis: percentage of income (%)
x-axis: percentage of population from poorest to richest (%)

 Articulation sentence:
The Gini coefficient and GDP per capita are two different ways of measuring a country's development based on their economic strength.

More complex measures of development

The debate about the economic and more **holistic** views of development also raises the question of how to best measure development if we do not use economic indicators.

More complex measures of development attempt to capture aspects of development other than just economic data. For example, the Human Development Index (HDI) combines data on life expectancy, education and income, while the Happy Planet Index (HPI) is an attempt to include more variables that measure the long-term impact on the environment. There are many different **indices**. However, the HDI is the most commonly used.

 Articulation sentences:
It is difficult to measure non-economic indicators of development. However, the Human Development Index is a popular method of measurement.

Theories and models of development

Modernization theory

Modernization theory is the oldest theory of development. It is based on the study of the economic history of industrialized Western nations, such as the United Kingdom, Germany and the United States. Modernization theory states that there is a single way for countries to modernize and develop – by **imitating** what the industrial countries did. Walt Whitman Rostow is the most well-known modernization theorist and described five distinct stages of development.

1   Traditional societies: Societies that are based on **subsistence agriculture**, with low levels of technology and pre-scientific values.

2   Preconditions for take-off: Societies that have started to introduce money and banking into their economy, and have a new class of entrepreneurs with scientific values.

3   Take-off: Societies in which values that encourage economic growth are widespread and growth of certain economic sectors has become common.

4   Drive to maturity: Societies with an economy that is diversifying and producing an increasingly large variety of goods. Standards are rising and poverty is decreasing.

5   High mass consumption: Societies in which wealth and the production and consumption of modern consumer goods are widespread.

When governments followed these ideas of development, they generally introduced policies that focused on the building of big infrastructure, the nurturing of new industries through national subsidies and investments, and the development of new trade relationships. The focus on industrialization also led to a serious city bias in some countries, with agricultural production being made as cheap as possible in order to feed growing city populations.

 Articulation sentence:

Modernization theory is based on the example of industrialized Western countries and suggests there is only one way for a country to develop.

Dependency theory

Dependency theory, also called World Systems theory, was popular during the 1960s and 1970s. It criticizes the assumptions of Modernization theory, the idea that underdeveloped countries simply need to copy what developed countries did in order to 'catch up'. Dependency theory has its roots in Marxism and focuses on the structure of the world economy as a whole, rather than on individual states. Here are the assumptions of dependency theory:

- Underdeveloped and newly independent states are locked into an unequal system of global trade, in which the already rich countries are set to benefit more, at the cost of poorer countries.

- The world is divided into a centre and a periphery. The centre consists of the former colonial powers and other Western industrialized countries. The periphery consists of the newly independent developing countries.

- The centre became rich by exploiting the periphery and has an interest in maintaining this unequal relationship in order to remain dominant in the world.

- It is difficult for all underdeveloped countries to simply 'catch up', as development of the industrialized West was based on the exploitation of others.

- The West has an interest in keeping exploited countries poorer.

The theory is a critique of the lack of development many countries experienced in the post-independence years. This is a typical model of what occurred. Governments in developing countries:

- placed high tariffs on imported consumer goods in order to protect their own industries;

- overvalued their currencies in order to make the import of production inputs cheaper;

- subsidized industries as well as agriculture in the interest of self-sufficiency.

The consequences of self-sufficiency and of cutting economic ties with former colonial powers were that it:

- led governments to borrow lots of money;
- led to corruption and money wasting as the state had a lot of power in regulating the economy;
- led to serious pressure by Western governments and international financial institutions (IFIs) on developing countries to change their development strategies, as debt crises of the 1970s had an impact on global economies.

Articulation sentences:

Dependency theory explained that underdeveloped nations could not copy Western nations in order to develop, because they were being exploited by them. This led underdeveloped countries to adopt expensive policies to protect their economies.

Neoliberalism

Neoliberalism replaced Dependency theory in the 1980s as the dominant world economic policy. It assumes that the free market is the most fair and efficient way to foster economic growth and development. According to this theory, government interference almost always has negative long-term consequences on development. This is because it can create sudden economic growth that does not last, and because corrupt officials have a lot of opportunities to take money for themselves illegally. A better solution would be to encourage free enterprise by intervening in the economy as little as possible. This would lead to healthy competition, meaning that only the strongest companies survive and grow, which in turn leads to sustainable long-term growth and development. Development should grow from Foreign Direct Investment, rather than government investment. Furthermore, the amount the state spends on public services such as healthcare and pensions should become smaller, so that people are encouraged to work and contribute to the economy. Two of the biggest supporters of these policies in the 1980s were Prime Minister Margaret Thatcher in the UK and President Ronald Reagan in the US.

Criticism

Many people say that neoliberalism removed the state from the development process – a lesson learned from the debt crises of the 1970s. The social cost of reducing government services would become the responsibility of private groups, such as charities and non-governmental organizations (NGOs), or would be lessened by paying private companies for services once provided by the state, for example in the health and education sectors. Thus, neoliberalism led to the beginning of privatization. Neoliberalism argues that healthy competition between social welfare providers leads to less corruption and more

Rich use money to pay for goods and services

Goods and service providers employ more people to meet demand

Unemployment decreases as more and more people benefit from the growing economy

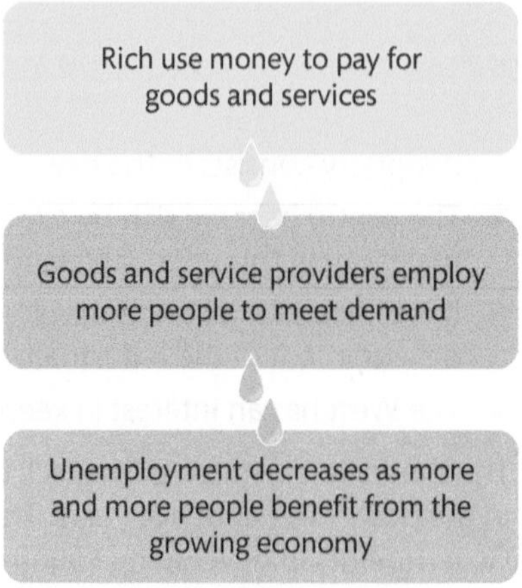

Fig 3.2 *Economy trickle-down diagram*

efficient use of resources. Neoliberalism also believes that newly created economic wealth will eventually 'trickle down' through all classes of society – as the rich get richer, they spend more money, which in turn helps various industries that employ more people to produce the consumer goods.

Consequences

In terms of policy, neoliberalism led to structural adjustment programmes (SAPs). These were **negotiated** between the IFIs, specifically the International Monetary Fund (IMF) and the World Bank on the one hand, and the governments of underdeveloped and **indebted** nations on the other hand. SAPs typically involved the lowering and eventual removal of trade barriers such as import tariffs, the devaluation of currencies, the cutting of public spending, such as subsidies, and the partial privatization of many public services, such as healthcare, education, waste management and sanitation. The results were mixed. Some countries emerged stronger after taking this '**bitter pill**', while others found themselves in a cycle of **stagnation** and inflation that crippled their national development further. SAPs were widely criticized for their harsh policies and the pressure that was put on governments to sign up to them, as a refusal to participate would often result in a cutting of any further aid or **credit**.

 Articulation sentences:
> Neoliberalism suggested that governments should not intervene in the economy, as the free market would allow for more competition and growth. SAPs were introduced to help indebted nations to grow, but they were only **beneficial** for some countries.

The Washington Consensus

In the 1990s, a lighter version of the neoliberalist **ideology** emerged, often referred to as the Washington Consensus. It has a stronger emphasis on free market non-interventionism, strong institutions and 'good policies'. This ideology tries to find a balance between complete **deregulation** and a strong and accountable government that manage the negative effects of liberalization. The Washington Consensus is pro-democracy and argues that free markets can only function effectively and efficiently in an environment where the rule of law is respected and citizens are able to express their opinions.

The Washington Consensus has influenced global development strategies such as the Millennium Development Goals (MDGs) and the Sustainable Development Goals (SDGs). It also guides the work of major players in the development field, such as the United Nations Development Programme, USAID and the World Bank.

 Articulation sentence:
> The Washington Consensus attempts to balance deregulation with an accountable government who oversee the market.

3.2 Key concept: Globalization

Key idea:

Globalization is a process of **interaction** and **integration**. It occurs between people, trading **entities** and governments of different nations.

The history of globalization

Globalization is a **by-product** of human movement and interaction. It first began when humans moved out of Africa into other parts of the world. When people travel and interact they take their ways of thinking, cultural **norms**, products and practices with them. These are borrowed, used and adapted by people they interact with.

CHALLENGE YOURSELF

Social and Communication skills ATL

In pairs, find examples of one country which prospered under the SAPs and one which struggled. Get together with another pair and, using your examples, discuss whether you believe SAPs were fair and effective.

General vocabulary

negotiated discussed something in order to reach an agreement, especially in business or politics

bitter pill an unpleasant fact or situation that is difficult to accept

globalization the idea that the world is developing a single economy and culture as a result of improved technology and communications and the influence of very large multinational companies

entities things that exist as single and complete units

norms the usual or normal situation; ways of doing something

Synonyms

indebted .... owing money

credit .... loans

beneficial ...... positive

interaction .... working together

integration .... greater connectivity

by-product ... consequence

Subject vocabulary

stagnation a situation in which a state's economy is not growing or succeeding

ideology opinions or beliefs, often linked to a particular political system or culture

deregulation removing government rules and controls from some types of business activity

Modern globalization is usually seen as being driven by international trade. However, it is also aided by other factors, as shown in Figure 3.3.

Figure 3.3 *Factors influencing globalization*

These developments allow modern people to interact and share ideas, goods and services on a larger scale, more easily and more frequently than in the past.

Types of globalization

Economic globalization

Economic globalization refers to the significant increase in the integration and **interdependence** of global economies. In practice this means a cross-border movement of services, products, money and technologies.

For example, the World Trade negotiations (Doha process) aimed to reduce tariffs and other barriers to trade between countries.

Political globalization

Political globalization refers to the increase of global **governance** beyond nation states. In practice this means a rise in influence for IGOs and NGOs. These are groups with specific aims and methods to tackle global problems such as climate change.

Intergovernmental organizations (IGOs) are organizations which are composed of nation states. Examples include the United Nations and the International Labour Organization. Non-governmental organizations (NGOs) are organizations which are neither part of a government nor a for-profit business. They can be funded by governments, **foundations**, businesses or individuals. Examples include Greenpeace and the World Wildlife Fund.

Cultural globalization

Cultural globalization refers to the increased sharing of ideas, meanings and values across the world. In practice this means a cross-border flow of cultural norms, values and media products (films, music, books, magazines and newspapers).

Examples include the increasing availability of video games, the popularity of Hollywood films, the influence of women's rights campaigns, children's rights campaigns, animal rights campaigns and global human rights, as well as the increased global use of English.

Articulation sentence:
There are different types of globalization: economic, political and cultural globalization.

CHALLENGE YOURSELF

 Research, Self-management and Communication skills

Cultural and political globalization can be linked. Look for a recent incident in which a pressure group, such as Amnesty International, used their influence to change the behaviour of a state. For example, you could research prisoners who have been released from Guantanamo Bay. Prepare a five-minute presentation of your research and present it to the class.

The impact of globalization

The impact on states

The impact of economic globalization has been the freer movement of capital, products and business ideas, and a greater access to cheaper labour. For example, American business ideas have been imported to China as the country moved towards a capitalist model; German cars are now built in Mexico (for example, Audi) because labour is cheaper there than in Germany.

The impact of political globalization has been to give citizens greater access to powerful groups outside of their own nation. These groups may have influence over nation states. For example, human rights abuses can be documented by the United Nations or the Red Cross and can be acted upon. Together with new technology, political globalization has also encouraged 'citizen journalism', which allows news stories to be reported worldwide by interest groups.

The impact of cultural globalization has been to give citizens access to rights, norms, beliefs, roles and expectations they would not ordinarily have access to in such large numbers. For example, American notions of 'individualism', femininity and the role and expectations of women have all reached a wide audience through the dominance of Hollywood films. The Hollywood film industry has also influenced the global notion, and appearance, of cityscapes and suburbia. They can become established as the norm and an ideal to aspire to, influencing the debates and future direction of other countries.

 Articulation sentence:

Economic globalization has affected states by allowing the freer movement of capital, products and business ideas, and a greater access to cheaper labour.

The impact on private groups

Economic globalization and cultural globalization have had an impact on national and multinational corporations by increasing trade and investment opportunities and spreading business ideas beyond a nation's borders. For example, after visiting the US, Chinese entrepreneur Jack Ma founded Alibaba. Alibaba is a China-based online marketplace which currently serves people in more than 240 countries and territories. It provides electronic payment services, a shopping search engine and cloud computing services. Alibaba provides consumer-to-consumer, business-to-consumer and business-to-business sales services through the internet. Ma has become one of the world's richest individuals.

Political globalization has had an impact on private groups by giving them access to international aid services and pressure groups. For example, the World Economic Forum (WEF) is a Swiss non-profit foundation. Aung San Suu Kyi announced on the World Economic Forum's website that she wanted to run for the presidency in Myanmar's 2015 elections. Aung San Suu Kyi is a politician from Myanmar and chairperson of the National League for Democracy (NLD) in Myanmar. She has used the WEF to promote awareness of the abuses taking place in Myanmar.

 Articulation sentence:

Economic globalization and cultural globalization have had an impact on national and multinational corporations by increasing trade and investment opportunities, and spreading business ideas beyond a nation's borders.

Synonyms

capital	money and property
labour	workers
documented	recorded
aspire to	want

Subject vocabulary

capitalist model an economic and political system in which a state's trade and industry are primarily controlled by private owners for profit without government interference

citizen journalism a process whereby events, stories and investigations are reported by people who are not professional journalists

suburbia relating to the suburbs; an outlying district of a city, especially a residential one

General vocabulary

abuses cruel or violent treatment

interest groups groups of people who join together to try to influence the government in order to protect their own particular rights or advantages

expectations feelings or beliefs about the way something should be or how someone should behave

cityscapes the way cities look

cloud computing the use of computer programs that are on the internet rather than on your own computer

pressure groups groups or organizations that try to influence the opinions of ordinary people and persuade the government to do something

The impact on culture

Economic globalization has had an impact on culture by giving people of different cultures access to ideas, products and services from other cultures, for example, **restaurant chains**, films and music, **social media**, and technology that allows access to social media.

Political globalization has had an impact on culture by requiring the promotion of cultural norms on a global **platform**. For example, the United Nations Human Rights Council (UNHRC) promotes and protects human rights around the world. The United Nations Refugee Agency, which protects **refugees**, encourages women to **empower** themselves in their communities and to participate fully in all decisions that affect their lives. This objective – empowering women to make key decisions – can cause misunderstanding or conflict in cultures where women are not considered to have equal **status** to men.

The impact of cultural globalization on culture is that world cultures are becoming more and more **homogenized**. Homogenization refers to an increase in Westernized culture around the world, such as the **prevalence** of Western music, films, consumer culture, Western cultural norms and the increased use of the English language. However, an alternative argument states that there is greater **hybridization** than is immediately apparent. Hybridization refers to the mixing of religious ideas and cultural norms and assumes there is less homogenization.

Articulation sentence:
> Globalization has had an impact on culture by giving members of different cultures access to ideas, products and services from other cultures.

The impact on global political interaction

Economic globalization has had an impact on global political interaction by reducing the potential for armed conflict. This is because national economies have become increasingly dependent on other nation states. For example, China is one of Japan's main export partners. The two countries sometimes have **tense diplomatic relations** concerning **territory**, and in the past they have been enemies. However, their trading relations are increasingly interlinked, and each country has significant sales and interests in the other. Any armed conflict would result in massive economic problems for both countries.

Political globalization has had an impact on global political interaction by forcing states to cooperate more on issues raised by IGOs and NGOs. For example, among others, the last UN High Commissioner for Refugees, António Guterres, has argued that women's rights should be a central policy for countries wishing to improve their development (Guterres, 2014). Improving women's rights has been shown to address issues as **diverse** as controlling birth rate, decreasing corruption, improving healthcare (especially for children), decreasing sexually transmitted disease **transmission rates**, reducing armed conflict and increasing the wealth of countries.

Increased global political interaction raises an issue of **accountability**. This is especially so in states where the issues raised by IGOs and NGOs are not necessarily being raised by their own citizens. Often these powerful IGOs and NGOs become skilful at using the forces of globalization to **further** their own interests and agendas. For example, improving women's rights may have many benefits to women and societies at large, but it can conflict with the cultural norms of many cultures.

Articulation sentence:
> Economic globalization has had an impact on global political interaction by reducing the potential for armed conflict, as national economies become increasingly dependent on other nation states.

3.3 Key concept: Inequality

Key idea:

It is now widely acknowledged that globalization has both advantages and disadvantages, and that its benefits are not evenly distributed. Inequality exists between countries and between various groups within countries as a result of globalization.

Advantages of globalization

- Increased economic growth: economies that have access to more markets, workers and resources are more likely to grow. This can mean more wealth for more people.
- Improved standards of living: workers who work within growing economies have more purchasing power and can access a wider variety of ideas, products and services.
- Globalized countries can become more democratic: economies that become more financially open usually have to become more politically open. Greater freedoms are enjoyed by people living in politically open states.
- Cultural development: globalized cultures tend to embrace modern ideas, for example, with regards to women's rights, children's rights, worker rights and the rights of other minority groups, such as LGBT and racial minorities.

Articulation sentence:

Globalization leads to access to a wider variety of ideas, products and services.

Disadvantages of globalization

- Growing wealth gap: in a globalized market place, wealth can become concentrated within an elite. For example, as Russia opened its energy markets, a small group of politically connected individuals (known as oligarchs) benefited, while the vast majority of Russians did not.
- Wage competition: workers have to compete with workers in other countries and this places pressure on wages. The result is potentially lower wages, as multinational corporations can threaten to relocate their factories to places with lower worker wages. This is good for corporate profits, but not for workers.
- Price competition: there is global price competition, meaning prices are sometimes lowered. However, the option to buy abroad is usually only of benefit to large corporations and not individuals (due to the cost of transporting goods from overseas).
- Regulation avoidance: corporations can locate factories in countries where regulations are less strict. Regulations might cover workers' rights, fire safety, health and safety, or child labour.
- Lack of cultural diversity: globalization does not always lead to an equal exchange of ideas, products and services. For example, English is becoming a dominant language. At the same time, Western corporations are dominant within many market places, while non-Western corporations go bankrupt as they find it difficult to compete.

Synonyms

acknowledged	accepted
embrace	welcome
vast	extremely large
wage	salary
regulation	official rules

Subject vocabulary

LGBT lesbian, gay, bisexual and transgender people

energy markets markets that deal specifically with the trade and supply of energy such as oil, gas and coal

General vocabulary

concentrated present in large numbers or amounts somewhere

elite a group of people who have a lot of power and influence because they have money, knowledge or special skills

relocate move to a new place

bankrupt without enough money to pay what you owe

CHALLENGE YOURSELF

Research and Thinking skills

Look up the Fairtrade Foundation. They aim to ensure workers receive fair pay. On their website you can read about the world sugar trade. Which countries are finding it difficult to trade sugar and why? Has globalization of the sugar trade benefited those countries?

Articulation sentences:

Globalization does not always lead to an equal distribution of benefits. For example, workers have to compete with workers in other countries and this places pressure on wages. This is good for corporate profits, but not for workers.

Example: The standard of living in rural India

Standard of living refers to the level of wealth, comfort, services and material goods that are available to a certain group in a certain geographic area.

- 65 per cent of India's population is rural, and 58 per cent of the rural labour force works in agriculture.
- More than 85 per cent of farmers own less than two hectares of land and are classed as small-scale farmers (Suneja, 2015).
- Small-scale farmers produce around 70 per cent of all vegetables, 55 per cent of fruits, 52 per cent of cereal and 69 per cent of milk (Dev, 2012). Yet they have only 44 per cent of the land area (Birthal, 2011).

Thus, small-scale farmers are essential to Indian food security and to the Indian economy.

India began to open its economy to global economic forces in the 1970s. It has removed government restrictions and allowed foreign investment. For example:

- The fertilizer cooperative IFFCO launched a joint venture with the Japanese firm Mitsubishi Corp. Together they manufacture agrochemicals in India.
- A Dutch-based private equity group, Rabo Equity Advisors, raised $100 million for a fund called India Agri Business Fund II. The fund plans to invest $15–17 million in 10 to 12 Indian agricultural companies.

Articulation sentences:

Globalization opened up the Indian rural economy. This meant Indian farmers, which were mostly small-scale, could access foreign technology and credit to improve their businesses. It also meant they could sell their products to more markets.

As the Indian economy grew, the GDP per person in India doubled from $260 in 1980 to $538 in 2003 (Pandey and Dixit, 2008). However, economic growth has not been evenly distributed among India's population:

- Even though India relies on small-scale farmers, 41.9 per cent of agricultural labour households are still categorized as poor (Singh, 2012).
- There is a significant difference between rural and urban areas: 25 per cent of the rural population is below the poverty line, while only 13.7 per cent of the urban population is below the poverty line (Reserve Bank of India, 2012).
- Rural wages do not grow as fast as urban wages. Rural wages are also more likely to change due to weather and changes in global prices for agricultural goods (Surabhi, 2015).
- In India in 2004–2005, women working on farms earned only 70 per cent of what men earned. Over 80 per cent of women did not get the minimum wage, compared with 41 per cent of men.
- The suicide rate among farmers is 47 per cent higher than the Indian national average (Indian census, 2011). The overwhelming majority of suicide victims are men.

Articulation sentences:

Globalization has placed pressure on small-scale farmers. There have been negative effects for the rural population, which are different for men and women.

In what ways does globalization cause inequalities in standards of living?

Less government protection for poorer people

Economic globalization places an emphasis on less government regulation. This led to Indian rural wages either falling or not **keeping pace** with the rest of the economy. The Indian government had to increase regulation in order to guarantee wages. This led to wage increases in agriculture, although only in some regions (Singh, 2012).

Influence of large-scale businesses

Articulation sentences:

Small-scale farmers are forced to compete with large-scale farming corporations in a more open market with less government protection. This negatively affects wages.

Small-scale farmers have:

- less access to capital;
- less access to public-funded services such as **canals**;
- less education, and so are at a disadvantage when it comes to negotiating favourable contracts and solving disagreements.

Large-scale farmers can:

- buy more fertile land and land near canals;
- use more machinery and hire fewer workers, which increases output and lowers production costs;
- have more access to expensive technology, such as fertilizer and refrigeration units;
- use lawyers to **settle** land **disputes** in their favour, and negotiate with foreign investors;
- access good quality credit, and then invest the money in their business;
- use **information and communication technology (ICT)** to **predict** market changes and communicate with suppliers and buyers;
- **absorb** price changes more easily;
- absorb the effects of climate change and other environmental challenges.

Articulation sentence:

Large-scale farmers have more access to credit and technology to overcome problems and expand their market share.

3.4 Key concept: Sustainability

Key idea:

Sustainability refers to the capacity of countries and groups to maintain themselves by reducing factors that threaten **well-being**.

Sustainability can be seen in terms of the Three **Pillars** of Sustainability, adopted by the 2005 World Summit on Social Development. They are economic sustainability, social sustainability and environmental sustainability. Cato (2009) has argued that the economy and society should be **constrained** by the environment. Therefore, the model can appear as in Figure 3.4.

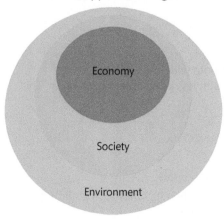

Figure 3.4 Cato's model of the Three Pillars of Sustainability

❝ Articulation sentences:
Economic sustainability aims to reduce factors that threaten economic well-being. Social sustainability aims to reduce factors that threaten human social well-being. Environmental sustainability aims to reduce factors that threaten environmental well-being.

Economic sustainability

Economic sustainability aims to reduce factors that threaten economic well-being. Strategies to address this may include:

- establishing sustainable transportation and infrastructure (e.g. roads, railways, air **freight**);
- investing in education, research, technology, **entrepreneurial** and **workforce** skills;
- increasing jobs and incomes through business development;
- reducing corruption.

Globalization can influence economic sustainability by:

- introducing new ideas that can improve the well-being of businesses;
- creating new opportunities which were not previously available (such as new markets);
- introducing new technologies (such as software applications, **tooling** for manufacturing and communication technologies);
- reducing tariffs between countries and establishing systems to ease **monetary flow** and access to market places.

Example: Addressing the North–South divide

The North–South divide refers to an economic and political divide between countries in the Northern **Hemisphere** and countries in the Southern Hemisphere.

The Global North includes the United States, Canada, Western Europe and developed parts of East Asia. The Global South includes Africa, Latin America and developing Asia, including the Middle East. Countries in the Global North are all members of the **G8** and make up four of the five permanent members of the United Nations Security Council. It is characterized by:

- technology, urban and manufacturing-based economies;
- low birth and death rates;
- relatively high levels of **empowerment** for women;
- low population density.

The Global South is characterized by:

- **agrarian**-based economies;
- high birth and death rates;
- relatively low levels of empowerment for women;
- high population density;
- economic and political dependence on the Global North (Odeh, 2010);
- low productivity, low income (Dasgupta and Ray,1987).

Addressing the North–South Divide can be achieved by:

- allowing the easier transfer of new technology and ideas from North to South;
- cancelling or **rescheduling** debts of the Global South;
- increasing the Global South's representation within global institutions, such as the World Bank, G8 and the UN Security Council;
- addressing the food crises of the Global South quicker and with more emphasis on sustainability;
- empowering women in the Global South.

> **Articulation sentences:**
> Countries in the Northern Hemisphere are considered more prosperous and powerful. Countries in the Southern Hemisphere have to obey rules set by those in the North and this can **inhibit** their development.

General vocabulary

hemisphere a half of the earth, especially one of the halves above or below the equator

empowerment having control over your own life or situation

agrarian relating to farming or farmers

rescheduling arranging for something to happen at a different time from the one that was previously planned

inhibit prevent something from growing or developing well

Subject vocabulary

G8 The Group of Eight (G8) refers to the group of eight highly industrialized nations: France, Germany, Italy, the United Kingdom, Japan, the United States, Canada and Russia, with representation for the European Union

population density the number of people living in a geographical space

Synonyms

prosperous .... wealthy

Social sustainability

Social sustainability aims to reduce factors that threaten human social well-being. Figure 3.5 shows some of the strategies used to address this.

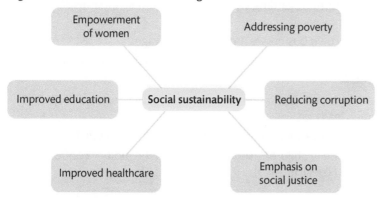

Figure 3.5 *Social sustainability diagram*

General vocabulary

caring professions jobs that involve helping others, such as nursing

contraception the practice of preventing a woman from becoming pregnant when she has sex, or the methods for doing this

privilege a special advantage that is given only to one person or group of people

literacy the state of being able to read and write

migration when large numbers of people go to live in another area or country, especially in order to find work

Example: The empowerment of women

Gender is an important part of identity. It is partially socially constructed and partially biologically determined. Gender roles are the behaviours associated with being a man or a woman and these are influenced by culture. Globalization can influence social sustainability by:

- introducing new ideas about the roles of men and women (such as women owning and running businesses; men working in the **caring professions**);
- creating new opportunities which were not previously available (such as businesses and services run by and for women);
- introducing new technologies, medical services and cultural norms (such as **contraception**).

 Articulation sentences:
Globalization can mean traditional gender roles are questioned. This is particularly true for the association of masculinity with **privilege**.

Many key aspects of global politics remain fundamentally affected by gender, for example human rights and health concerns. Issues such as **literacy**, **migration**, sexual violence and disease continue to have a different impact on men, women and children because of cultural norms associated with men and women.

 Articulation sentence:
Issues such as literacy, migration, sexual violence and disease continue to have a different impact on men, women and children because of different cultural norms.

The empowerment of women is an important part of social sustainability. According to Barber Conable, former president of the World Bank, women do 70 per cent of the world's work but only earn 10 per cent of the world's income. This leads to greater poverty, slower economic growth and a lower standard of living for the entire community.

The UN agreed Millennium Development Goals in 2000 to formalize a set of global targets for development across the world, working to achieve these by 2015. Millennium Development Goal 3 is to promote gender equality and empower women. It is assumed the empowerment of women has beneficial effects for all community members.

Empowerment of women can be achieved by:

- educating girls;
- changing cultural stereotypes and expectations for women;
- challenging social norms regarding women (such as **female infanticide** and lack of education);
- allowing women to own businesses and earn equal wages;
- allowing women to have access to cultural, social, economic and political positions of power.

The empowerment of women has a significant effect on social sustainability. Empowering women leads to:

- a higher proportion of earnings **reinvested** in the family (OECD, 2012);
- a 20 per cent increase in children's survival rate when the mother controls household income (Zoellick, 2010);
- less corruption;

- women taking control of their bodies which:
  - reduces the birth rate;
  - reduces the early marriage rate;
  - reduces the HIV infection rate (as women insist on more use of contraception);
  - results in more girls finishing school and becoming economically active, rather than becoming young mothers (OECD, 2012).

Environmental sustainability

Environmental sustainability aims to reduce factors that threaten environmental well-being. It usually focuses on land use, atmosphere, food production and energy use. Figure 3.6 shows some strategies to address this.

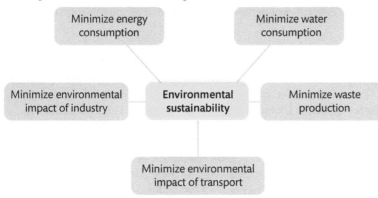

Figure 3.6 *Environmental sustainability diagram*

The economies of the Global North have grown significantly at the expense of the environment. The Global South wants to copy the economic success of the Global North. However, this causes tensions because the Global North now wants to encourage environmental protection, which is often not a priority for the Global South. The Global North is more powerful economically and politically than the Global South and it can impose restrictions on the economies of countries that damage the environment.

 Articulation sentences:
The Three Pillars of Sustainability should not be seen in isolation. They interact with one another.

Example: Economic growth and environmental degradation

Economies have a significant effect on environmental sustainability. It is often the case that as economies grow, the environment degrades (Adams and Jeanrenaud, 2008). It is argued that economic and environmental sustainability is currently balanced in the developing world, despite the high population density. However, as the economies in the developing world grow, more people will adopt a Western lifestyle. Western lifestyles are characterized by high consumption and high waste production.

It can also be noted that as developing countries adopt Western cultural norms, there is greater female empowerment leading to a lower birth rate.

4.1 Key concept: Peace

Key idea:

Peace is the absence of violence or **conflict**, sometimes **underpinned** by a level of deeper **equity** and **harmony**.

What is peace?

Peace is the absence of violent conflict. However, analysing whether a society, state or region is in a sustainable state of peace requires deeper examination. It cannot be determined simply by visible evidence, such as the absence of violent **confrontation**. Measuring a state of peace depends on a deeper assessment of the absence of violence, but also the deeper level of harmony that a society, state or region enjoys.

Negative peace

Negative peace involves merely the absence of active, organized violence by both state and non-state groups. Violent conflict may have been absent for many years (in more stable states) or it may have ended very recently (for example, in **ceasefires** and **truces**, such as the ceasefire agreed in Ukraine by the Minsk Agreement in 2015 or during the Northern Ireland **peace process** in the 1990s). This assessment of peace looks no deeper. It does not consider the factors contributing to non-violence. This concept of peace is most useful at the first stage in conflict **resolution**, when the aim is to stop immediate violence. It is possible to analyse whether an apparently stable state, such as the United States, is truly in a state of negative peace. Racial **tensions** and violent **clashes**, such as the violence in 2014 in Ferguson, Missouri, may suggest otherwise.

Positive peace

Positive peace looks more deeply at what helps sustain peace beyond simply reducing or stopping violence. It is possible to identify a deeper level of harmony in society, where the causes of conflict themselves are **neutralized**, rather than violence merely absent. Here, there is no visible violence and no deeper social causes of conflict. Society is **just** and equal. Former enemies make peace and each has an equal **stake in** society. For example, efforts to build sustainable peace in Somalia in 2012 re-established a representative parliament and agreed a new national **constitution**. The aim was to create political equality in Somalia by giving all **clans** a voice. Efforts were made to **reintegrate** former **militants**, who had renounced violence, back into society. In the Northern Ireland peace process, the Good Friday Agreement in 1998 created a **power-sharing executive** involving all political parties.

> Articulation sentence:
> Peace is the absence of conflict; it can be either positive – with the long-term causes of conflict resolved sustainably – or negative – meaning there is an absence of violence.

Theoretical viewpoints

	Negative peace	Positive peace
Realist view	The more natural state in an anarchical world order. States exist to protect and advance their own national interests. Their priority is national security over peace for its own sake.	An unrealistic aim. It is natural for states to compete with each other. Equal status among nation states is both impossible and undesirable.
Liberal view	A desirable and realistic first objective, perhaps to be achieved through diplomacy, negotiation and with the assistance of IGOs. A means to an end, rather than an end in itself.	The desired final state in all conflict situations, seen as realistic and achievable. Both sides will be willing to make big concessions on core interests and seek to reconcile and forgive.

$$Peace = \frac{Equity + Harmony}{Violence + Trauma}$$

Figure 4.1 *Galtung peace formula*

Norwegian peace theorist, Johan Galtung (b.1930), suggests that there are four key components that influence the presence or absence of peace. He links them to specific tasks required to develop positive peace. Galtung suggests that peace processes should focus on the dual task of increasing equity and harmony, while reducing violence and trauma.

Equity

A society must operate on the basis of equality in order to have peace. There must be political equality, in which all adult citizens have the right to vote and participate in the political system. There must be economic equality, with equal opportunities and access to resources. Finally, there must be equality before the law – every citizen is equal before the law and no citizen or institution is above the law.

Examples

Newly created democratic institutions may be designed so that all political parties are involved in government through a system of power sharing. For example the Northern Ireland Assembly was created in 1998 after the Good Friday Agreement. The main Republican and Unionist parties share executive power. This peace process also reformed Northern Ireland's police force, ensuring greater representation of Catholics in a previously Protestant-dominated police force.

Harmony

Harmony is the hardest to measure of all the components of a peaceful society. A harmonious society is one in which all individuals within a society work together despite differences of race, ethnicity, class or caste, religion, gender, sexual orientation or age. After conflict, harmony may be increased through national processes such as Truth and Reconciliation Commissions, which expose wrongdoing and promote forgiveness and reconciliation. Harmony can be measured through opinion polls, which reveal public attitudes and tolerance of minorities.

INCREASE

Subject vocabulary

anarchical lacking any rules or order, or not following the rules of society

concessions something you give or allow to someone in order to reach an agreement

Truth and Reconciliation Commissions a commission tasked with discovering and revealing past wrongdoing by a government (or sometimes non-state groups), in the hope of resolving conflict left over from the past

General vocabulary

means to an end a way of getting or achieving something that you want

reconcile find a way to make ideas, beliefs or needs that are opposed to each other capable of existing together

trauma a bad experience that makes you feel very upset, afraid or shocked

resources something such as useful land, or minerals such as oil or coal, that exists in a country and can be used to increase its wealth

institution a large organization that has a particular kind of work or purpose

above the law allowed to not obey the law

ethnicity the country or tribe someone comes from

caste one of the fixed social classes, which cannot be changed, into which people are born in India

sexual orientation the fact that someone is heterosexual or homosexual

reconciliation a situation in which people, groups or countries become friendly with each other again after quarrelling

Synonyms

dual .... double

polls .... surveys

Examples

Truth and Reconciliation Commissions were established in Sierra Leone (2004), Liberia (2009) and Colombia (2015). Laws and constitutions may be created or adapted to protect against discrimination and prejudice. For example, South Africa's post-apartheid constitution guarantees equality before the law and freedom from discrimination.

Violence

Violence is physical or psychological harm. This can be caused either by physical force by groups in conflict, or by structures within society or government (such as violence against women under the Taliban in Afghanistan), causing injury, damage or death.

Examples

If both sides in a conflict agree to a ceasefire or truce, violence may be reduced. For example, in 2014, the Minsk Protocol was agreed between the parties involved in the eastern Ukraine conflict. Both sides agreed to a ceasefire, which was monitored by independent international observers from an IGO, the Organization for Security and Cooperation in Europe (OSCE). The decommissioning of weapons, defined as putting weapons in a position where they can no longer be used, may also be an aim of a ceasefire or truce. For example, an independent commission confirmed in 2005 that the Irish Republican Army had decommissioned the 'totality of its weapons', making a return to violence less likely.

Trauma

Trauma is the emotional shock following the stress of conflict or violence. This can lead to long-term distress and harm, bitterness and grievance between parties that were in conflict. Grievances left unresolved are likely to cause a return to conflict.

Examples

Emotional trauma, in terms of the bitterness and resentment that conflict creates, may be reduced by either retributive justice or restorative justice. International courts such as the International Criminal Court have convicted leaders responsible for crimes against humanity in the conflict in Democratic Republic of Congo. By 2016, the International Criminal Tribunal for the Former Yugoslavia, established by the UN Security Council in 1993, was still hearing evidence for war crimes committed since the late 1990s. Prisoners from both sides of the conflicts in Northern Ireland (1998) and Colombia (2015) have been released and granted amnesty.

Articulation sentence:
Galtung suggests that peace processes should focus on increasing equity and harmony, and reducing violence and trauma.

Peace and power

Power plays an important role in developing peace, notably in the distribution and balance of power between great powers who might be drawn into conflict with each other. Power may be used by one state alone (unipolarity), or by two rivals (bipolarity) or distributed among many states (multipolarity) and non-state groups. Identifying which global order is dominant at any one time is complex, as is whether one or the other is more or less likely to produce peace.

DECREASE

Unipolarity

In a unipolarity, one great power or hegemon exists which cannot be challenged militarily by any other. Realists call this hegemonic stability theory – the absolute power and dominance of the hegemon makes conflict less likely. Sceptics suggest that while immediate conflict is unlikely, in the long term conflict may result as other powers seek to remove power from the hegemon. However, truly global hegemons are extremely rare and are more likely to exist at regional, rather than global, level.

Bipolarity

In the Cold War, the United States and Soviet Union were in direct bipolar competition with each other, but never fought each other directly. The appalling consequences of nuclear war introduced a measure of stability, so-called mutually assured destruction. However, during the Cold War there was prolonged regional instability with proxy wars, in which both powers challenged each other by fighting with or against third parties. For example, there were long conflicts in Vietnam and Afghanistan.

Multipolarity

Many analysts agree that the current world order is multipolar. Many powers are competing with each other and non-state groups (for example, Islamic State in Syria and Iraq, and Boko Haram in Nigeria) are challenging nation states in armed conflict. Realists believe there is more instability in a multipolar order. Liberals, meanwhile, are more optimistic. They believe if many states have power, it increases the possibility of nation states working together in the common interest. For example, they work together through international organizations such as the United Nations, whose core goal is international peace.

Democratic peace theory

Some theorists believe that democracy itself promotes peace. They note that conflict between democratic states is rare. It is suggested that in democratic states, there is a fairer balance of power and distribution of wealth and resources. This internal stability reduces potential sources of grievance. It also promotes dispute resolution through democratic rather than violent means, because the previous success of democratic models of conflict resolution makes it clearer to all how conflict can be avoided in the future. For example, in 2012 the national parliament was re-established in Somalia. This institution allows members to resolve disputes through dialogue, in a format that had not existed during the country's civil war. Therefore, introducing democracy is often a key part of peacebuilding efforts, though it is no guarantee of stability. The lengthy military campaigns in Afghanistan (2001–2014) and Iraq (2003–2011), led by the United States, created new democratic institutions. However, these were continually threatened by violent insurgent attacks.

> **Articulation sentence:**
> Power can be unipolar (focused in one state), bipolar (divided between two states) or multipolar (split between several states or organizations).

Subject vocabulary

hegemon a state so powerful that it dominates all other states in the system, global or regional

hegemonic stability theory when one state is so powerful that others are unlikely to challenge it, and therefore there is no conflict

mutually assured destruction when both sides in a conflict would be able to inflict terrible damage on each other

proxy war a war started by a major power, where smaller powers or groups do the fighting on behalf of the major power

insurgent one of a group of people fighting against the government of their own country, or against authority

Synonyms

appalling .... terrible

The security dilemma

Realists believe that strong national security and defence are a priority because they protect a state from potential aggressors and secure power over its competitors. Critics argue that as a state builds up its defences, this may be interpreted by other states as aggressive. Other states may then respond by building up their own military forces. This means the military resources available to both states increase. The result for both states is greater insecurity, the opposite of the original goal. Some analysts observed this dilemma when former Soviet states in Eastern Europe joined NATO after the Cold War. For example, Ukraine – bordering Russia – planned to join NATO. Russia considered this a threat to its national security. This contributed to Russian military intervention in the Crimea region of Ukraine in 2014, as Russia wanted to secure its Black Sea fleet.

Pathways to peace

There are three main ways that regions, states and societies build peace. They happen in **sequence**, and are therefore strongly linked to and dependent on each other.

Figure 4.2 *Key activities involved in moving towards positive peace*

Peacemaking

Peacemaking is stopping violent conflict and creating negative peace. A pause or end to immediate violence is achieved, commonly through negotiation. Pausing violence may allow for further **mediation** or negotiation and the building of trust between both sides in a conflict. The original causes of conflict will not yet be resolved, but a pause in violence enables **stabilization**, for example through a ceasefire or truce.

Colombia's largest left-wing **rebel** group, the FARC, agreed to a series of ceasefires as it negotiated with the Colombian government in 2015. Similarly, agreements between pro-Russian rebels and Ukrainian nationalist forces resulted in fragile ceasefires in eastern Ukraine in 2014, as they explored a long-term solution.

Peacekeeping

Peacekeeping is sustaining negative peace to allow positive peace to be built. When a ceasefire is agreed, independent peacekeepers may be sent to the area. They will ensure that the peace holds, allowing positive peace to be built. The priority is **monitoring** agreements made during the peacemaking process. This may be done by **armed forces** from an international or regional body such as the United Nations (UN) or **African Union** (AU), or by unarmed monitors from an organization such as the Organization for Security and Cooperation in Europe (OSCE).

Peacekeeping continues to be a major activity for the United Nations. Since 2000, UN peacekeepers have been sent mainly to Africa, including to the Democratic Republic of Congo (established 2010) and Sudan's Darfur region (established 2007). These missions are always **legitimized** by a UN Security Council **resolution**. The number of nations that send troops on these peacekeeping missions has increased considerably in recent years. They include states that have recently emerged from conflict themselves, such as Sierra Leone, which in 2012 sent peacekeepers to the African Union mission to Somalia.

General vocabulary

sequence a series of related events or actions that happen or are done in a particular order

stabilization making something firm and steady

rebel someone who opposes or fights against people in authority

armed forces a country's military organizations, including the army, navy and air force

legitimized made official or legal

Subject vocabulary

mediation try to end a quarrel between people, groups or states

African Union a regional IGO of which most African states are members, focusing primarily on security and economic prosperity

resolution a formal decision or statement agreed on by a group of people, especially after a vote

Synonyms

monitoring .... checking

CHALLENGE YOURSELF

 Thinking and Research skills

Find out about the UN's peacekeeping activities in Cyprus. How long have there been UN peacekeepers in the country? What does this tell you about the nature of peacekeeping?

Peacebuilding

Peacebuilding is the building of sustainable, positive peace and long-term conflict resolution. This includes stabilization efforts to build longer-lasting peace and security, in order to achieve positive peace. Commonly, it involves significant development assistance to improve health and education, address inequality and rebuild destroyed infrastructure. It may also involve deeper reconciliation efforts, such as Truth and Reconciliation Commissions, amnesties or trials for war criminals.

Many peacekeeping missions approved by the UN have a specific mandate to carry out peacebuilding activities alongside traditional peacekeeping. Recent interventions in Afghanistan under NATO (2001–2014) and in Iraq under the US-led coalition (2003–2011) developed into major peacebuilding projects (sometimes known as nation building, where the entire structures of a nation state require rebuilding from complete destruction). When peacebuilding troops left Afghanistan in 2014, there had been 9 per cent economic growth. Healthcare provision had increased to 60 per cent from 9 per cent. There were also 2.5 million more girls in education and the first peaceful transfer of power since 1901 had taken place. However, considerable security problems still remained.

 Articulation sentences:

> There are three stages to creating peace. Peacemaking happens to end conflict, peacekeeping aims to maintain the established peace and peacebuilding attempts to create long-lasting peace.

Truth and Reconciliation Commissions

Truth and Reconciliation Commissions (TRCs) aim to expose the wrongdoing of all those involved in a conflict in a way that promotes forgiveness and understanding, rather than punishment and recrimination. This kind of reconciliation involves accepting the status quo, agreeing and publicizing accounts of the conflict, understanding opposing views, and ultimately rebuilding relationships. South Africa and Sierra Leone are powerful examples of successful Truth and Reconciliation Commissions. Both achieved a balance between restorative justice and retributive justice. In both cases, the news and events were highly publicized and televised. They published very detailed reports exposing wrongdoing and making recommendations for the future. Such commissions are rare. These two examples relied on a deeply religious culture and a strong belief in forgiveness (the South African commission was chaired by Archbishop Desmond Tutu and hearings began with prayers). Both also occurred once the previous government had left power and both nations were in a conscious process of rebuilding.

Peace through justice

In some conflicts, where there have been war crimes or genocide, war criminals have been prosecuted in special courts. Before the International Criminal Court opened in 2002, special tribunals were authorized by the UN Security Council. As of 2015, the International Criminal Tribunal for the Former Yugoslavia (ICTY) had sentenced 74 individuals for war crimes committed during the conflicts between 1991 and 2001. The International Criminal Court (ICC) was established by the Rome Statute in 1998 as a permanent international court for crimes against humanity. As of 2015, the court had made two convictions, both from the Democratic Republic of Congo.

 Articulation sentence:

> Usually after a conflict, intergovernmental organizations will attempt to build peace through Truth and Reconciliation Commissions and by prosecuting war criminals.

General vocabulary

infrastructure the basic systems and structures that a state or organization needs in order to work properly, for example roads, railways and banks

recrimination when you blame or criticize someone for something that has happened

status quo the state of a situation as it is

prosecuted charged with a crime and tried to show that they are guilty of it in a court of law

Subject vocabulary

mandate an official instruction given to a person or organization, allowing them to do something

nation building rebuilding an entire state and all its institutions

hearings meetings of a court or special committee to find out the facts about a case

genocide the deliberate murder of a whole group or race of people

4.2 Key concept: Conflict

Key idea:

Conflict is when parties disagree or compete with each other over ideas, resources or territory. Conflict may be violent or non-violent.

What is conflict?

Conflict is fundamentally about disagreement and competition over power, ideas, identity, resources or territory. The broadest definition of conflict covers a wide spectrum, including peaceful disagreement (for example, **strikes**) in its mildest form, to violent conflict involving many state and non-state groups (for example, the conflict in Syria which began in 2011).

Non-violent conflict	Violent conflict
Peaceful demonstrations	Terrorist attacks
Strikes	Civil war
Civil disobedience	Interstate war
Political campaigns	Insurgency or guerrilla war
Diplomacy	Genocide

 Articulation sentence:
Conflict is a disagreement, which can either be peaceful or violent.

Non-violent conflict

Not all conflict involves violence. In global politics, groups often disagree with each other in an entirely peaceful way, without violence. These conflicts are non-violent for a number of reasons.

- A legitimate structure or process for dialogue is in place, and everyone involved is using this.
- Democratic structures allow the population to be consulted. The results of these consultations are considered legitimate.
- The parties involved in the dispute are dependent on each other and would be harmed if the dispute became violent.
- Violent solutions are against the core interests of all parties.

Dispute	Non-violent conflict and resolution
Iran nuclear weapons programme	Conflict of ideas and security interests between nation states may be resolved through diplomacy and negotiation. In 2015, Iran and the United States (and the so-called P5+1, the permanent members of the UN Security Council plus Germany) disagreed over Iran's nuclear weapons programme. In 2015, Iran and the P5+1 used diplomacy and negotiation to discuss their conflicting interests and priorities, rather than violent conflict. As a result, economic sanctions were relaxed in exchange for weapons inspections. However, at times during the negotiations the threat of military action by the United States endangered the progress of the process.

Dispute	Non-violent conflict and resolution
European Union and the Eurozone crisis	The European Union was founded with the objective of creating a forum where European states could work together and resolve differences peacefully, through regional institutions. Integration reached an even deeper level with the launch of the euro in 2002, the European Union's single currency. New institutions, including a European Central Bank, were set up to manage monetary policy for the new currency. After the 2008 financial crisis, the Greek government requested loans from other Eurozone countries in order to pay its debts. Greece and other Eurozone countries frequently disagreed on the austerity measures Greece should take to stabilize its economy. All member countries share common institutions and interests, which means disputes can be resolved non-violently through discussion.
Scottish independence	In 2011, the Scottish National Party (SNP) won a majority in elections to the Scottish Parliament, a regional assembly with limited autonomy. The SNP had promised to hold a referendum on Scotland gaining independence from the United Kingdom and becoming an independent country. The dispute between pro-independence nationalists and anti-independence Unionists was resolved through a democratic referendum of the Scottish people. There was huge interest in the vote, with many young voters getting involved in the arguments for and against independence. In September 2014, a majority rejected independence and Scotland remains part of the United Kingdom.

 Articulation sentence:

Conflicts can be non-violent, often because states or groups are able to resolve their problems without violence and because they are dependent on one another.

Violent conflict

Much conflict results in violence. The most obvious form of violence in conflict is direct violence which can be measured by the numbers of people killed or injured, and by measuring the physical damage to infrastructure. Commonly, this type of violence takes place during a war. These conflicts can be violent for several reasons.

- Lack of trust between both sides of the conflict.
- No structure exists for the dispute to be resolved peacefully, through dialogue or democratic means.
- Grievance and trauma are sustaining, and deepening, the conflict.
- Violent approaches are seen as the only way to secure core interests.

CHALLENGE YOURSELF

Communication, Social and Research skills

In groups, find another example of a recent global non-violent conflict that has now been resolved. Make notes on the history of the issue and what was done to resolve the problem. Create a presentation of your research and explain your findings to the rest of the class.

Subject vocabulary

austerity when a government has a deliberate policy of trying to reduce the amount of money it spends

Synonyms

assembly .... government

autonomy ..... independence

General vocabulary

referendum when people vote in order to make a decision about a particular subject, rather than voting for a person or political party

Dispute	Violent conflict
Kurdistan and Turkey	Kurdish **separatist** forces have been fighting an insurgency against the Turkish Army in south-eastern Turkey. The main rebel group is the Kurdistan Workers' Party (known as the PKK), which wants to create a separate Kurdish state. Several ceasefires have failed and violent conflict has restarted. The conflict began in the late 1970s and since then approximately 45,000 people have been killed.
Ukraine	Violent conflict has been frequent in Ukraine. There are tensions because the people and its leadership are trying to decide between closer relations with the European Union and NATO to the west, or Russia to the east. In February 2014, there were violent protests in Kiev against President Viktor Yanukovych's pro-Russian stance and reversal of closer ties with the European Union. Security forces clashed with protesters in Independence Square, Kiev, and close to 100 protesters were killed. President Yanukovych **fled** to Russia and was replaced by pro-EU President Petro Poroshenko. In September 2014, Russian troops invaded eastern Ukraine and **annexed** the Crimea region. Protests in eastern Ukraine then developed into an armed insurgency between pro-Russian rebels, Russian forces and Ukrainian nationalist forces.
Syria	Civil war began in Syria in 2011 after initially peaceful protesters were shot at by government forces. By the end of 2015, 250,000 people had been killed in the conflict and much of Syria's physical infrastructure was destroyed. The UN has confirmed that in August 2013, government forces used chemical weapons in an attack on Damascus. One of the insurgent groups, Islamic State, has executed Western aid workers and journalists in Syria.

Articulation sentence:
Conflict can become violent when states or groups have no other means of resolving their disputes or because the conflict has been progressively getting worse.

Causes of conflict

In societies where there is conflict, it is possible to identify both specific causes and more general conditions that make conflict more likely. There is rarely just one single cause or condition. By the very nature of conflict, different sides in a conflict will not agree on the causes. Therefore, political analysts need to take care to analyse the possible causes in a balanced manner.

Galtung (1996) suggests that attitudes, behaviours and **contradictions** act together to encourage violent conflict. All three factors must be present for a full conflict to exist. Each factor **reinforces** the others. All three need to be stopped in order for conflict to end. If only one factor exists, then conflict may be likely to develop over time.

For example, violent behaviour will deepen contradiction. This may **harden** attitudes and deepen a sense of grievance or injustice. Peacekeeping can help reduce behaviours that encourage conflict. Peacebuilding can help reduce contradictions. Peacemaking can change the attitudes that fuel conflict.

In Galtung's model, violent conflict can be analysed at the manifest and latent levels. The manifest level is the immediately obvious evidence of violent conflict, for example the number of people killed or injured. The latent level is where the deeper causes and conditions of conflict can be analysed. It is important to remember that Galtung's conflict triangle applies to both violent and non-violent conflict.

Synonyms

manifest .... obvious

latent .... hidden

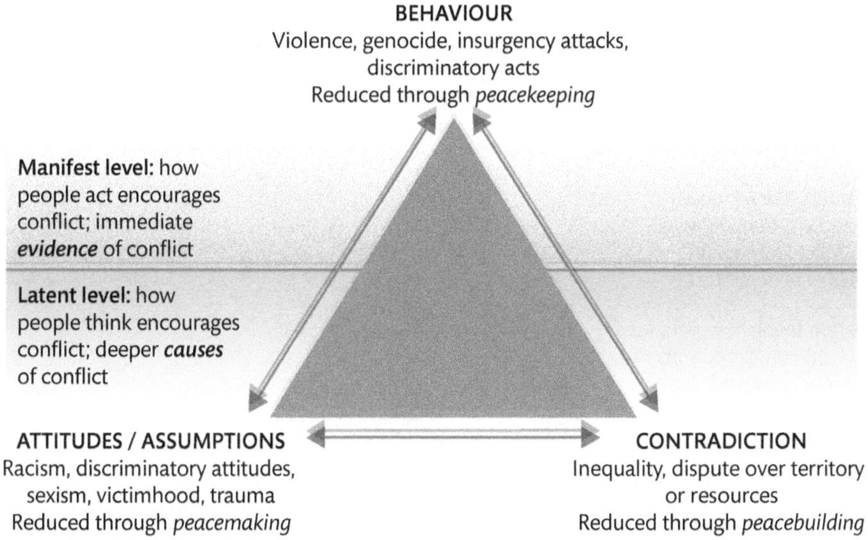

BEHAVIOUR
Violence, genocide, insurgency attacks, discriminatory acts
Reduced through *peacekeeping*

Manifest level: how people act encourages conflict; immediate *evidence* of conflict

Latent level: how people think encourages conflict; deeper *causes* of conflict

ATTITUDES / ASSUMPTIONS
Racism, discriminatory attitudes, sexism, victimhood, trauma
Reduced through *peacemaking*

CONTRADICTION
Inequality, dispute over territory or resources
Reduced through *peacebuilding*

Figure 4.3 *Galtung's conflict triangle*

Conditions making violent conflict more likely	Conditions making violent conflict less likely
Little or no democratic means of dispute resolution; minorities excluded from political representation	Democratic institutions exist, with full political equality and participation
Wealth, territory or resources shared unequally and controlled by powerful elites	Equal sharing of wealth and resources
Poverty	Equality of opportunity for all
Government is above the law, making arbitrary and illegitimate decisions	Government respects the rule of law
Judicial system is absent or interfered with, not independent or fair	Disputes can be resolved fairly through a fair and independent judicial system
Human rights are abused	Respect for human rights (especially of minorities)

General vocabulary

caliphate a single Islamic state, uniting many countries with Muslim populations into one much larger state unified by political and religious association with Islam

Using Galtung's methodology, it is possible to create a conflict triangle for contemporary conflicts, in order to analyse what is encouraging conflict. Figure 4.4 is an example for the violent conflict in Syria.

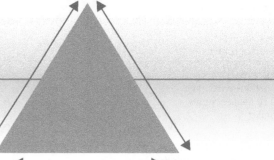

BEHAVIOUR
Assad government: military campaign against insurgency, chemical weapon attacks (August 2013)
Sunni rebel forces: violent insurgency campaign against the Assad government
Islamic State: military campaign to establish Sunni Islamic **caliphate**, fought against Shia Muslims and *Assad government*; execution of Western journalists

Manifest level: how people act encourages conflict; immediate *evidence* of conflict.

Latent level: how people act encourages conflict; deeper *causes* of conflict.

ATTITUDES / ASSUMPTIONS
Assad government believes it should stay in power, that rebel forces are 'terrorists' challenging the legitimate authority of the state. Sunni rebels feel Assad government is not legitimate, demanding greater representation and political equality, Sunnis marginalized by Assad's Shia-led government.

CONTRADICTION
Sunni majority is in conflict with the President's Shia Alawite sect, which has drawn in Sunni and Shia regional powers. Sunnis feel marginalized by Assad's Shia-led government. Islamic State believes it is legitimate to create a Sunni Muslim caliphate across Iraq and Syria, and does not accept international borders as currently defined.

Figure 4.4 *Galtung's conflict triangle for Syria*

> Articulation sentences:
> It is possible to identify both specific causes and more general conditions that make conflict more likely. Galtung's triangle is a method for analysing the causes of a conflict.

Types of conflict and groups involved in conflict

Different types of conflict exist, depending on two key factors.

- The nature of the groups involved – for example, nation states or non-state groups.
- The contradiction that is the cause of the conflict – for example, ideology, revolution, violent organized crime, or dispute over territory or resources.

Intrastate war has increased since 1946 and now represents the most common form of violent conflict.

Interstate war has decreased steadily since 1946. Particularly since the end of the Cold War, some years (for example, between 2004 and 2008) have seen no interstate war, anywhere in the world.

Subject vocabulary

ideology opinions or beliefs, often linked to a particular political system or culture

Synonyms

intrastate ...... within one state

Conflict and type	Group involved	Contradiction causing conflict
Afghanistan 2001–2014 State-led conflict against state and non-state groups (Taliban and al-Qaeda).	United States, NATO-mandated International Security Assistance Force, Taliban (ethnically Pashtun forces), al-Qaeda, Northern Alliance (ethnically Tajik forces).	United States began War on Terror. Taliban government refused to surrender al-Qaeda leader, Osama bin Laden, and to deny giving al-Qaeda safe operating space in Afghanistan. US and its allies removed Taliban from power and sought to degrade and destroy al-Qaeda, and bring bin Laden to justice.
Iraq 2003–2011 Interstate conflict between United States and Iraq under leadership of President Saddam Hussein. From 2004, asymmetric conflict between United States and Sunni insurgent non-state groups.	United States-led coalition without UN Security Council approval, Iraqi Army under leadership of Saddam Hussein, later against Sunni insurgent groups, principally al-Qaeda in Iraq (AQI).	United States accused Saddam Hussein of failure to comply with UN weapons inspections. US claims that suspected weapons of mass destruction (WMD) represent international security threat, justifying regime change. From 2004, Sunni insurgency developed in opposition to prolonged presence of US troops in Iraq.
Mexico 2006–present Conflict between violent organized criminals and Mexican government.	Mexican government and law enforcement agencies. Organized drug cartels, such as the Sinaloa Cartel, the world's largest drug-trafficking organization in the world.	Mexican security forces are fighting to control drug-related violence in Mexico, where cartels fight for control of trafficking routes.
Sri Lanka 1983–2009 Civil war of secession between Tamil Tigers and Sri Lankan government.	Liberation Tigers of Tamil Eelam and Sri Lankan state.	The Tamil Tigers fought an insurgency against the Sri Lankan state for an independent Tamil state in the north of Sri Lanka. The government defeated the Tamil Tigers in a long battle in the north of Sri Lanka, after which the Tamils surrendered.

Subject vocabulary

asymmetric conflict when two parties are fighting each other and one has superior resources compared to the other

regime change a change in the government of a country that happens because another country forces that government out of power

cartels a group of people or companies who agree to sell something at a particular price in order to prevent competition and increase profits

trafficking the buying and selling of illegal goods, especially drugs

secession when a country or state officially stops being part of another country and becomes independent

Articulation sentences:

Interstate war happens between states, but it has been decreasing since 1946. Intrastate war happens within one nation and is increasing.

How is conflict changing?

Many analysts have observed important changes in the nature of violent conflict, particularly since the end of the Cold War. A key method of analysis has been to observe the differences between 'old wars', based on interstate conflict, and 'new wars', based on new globalized conflicts between civilian and non-state groups, as notably proposed by Mary Kaldor (1999).

Old wars	New wars
Principal groups involved were regular armed forces of nation states.	Principal groups now involved are non-state groups, rebel groups and independent militia.
Fought for ideology or geopolitical interests.	Fought for identity – religious, ethnic, tribal.
Violence directed against and between national armed forces.	Violence directed against civilians.
Financed by states (taxation or outside support).	Financed by non-state groups exploiting local economies and by violent organized crime.
Emphasis on battles to capture territory.	Emphasis on controlling populations, displacing minorities.

❝ Articulation sentence:
> The nature of conflicts has been steadily changing from wars based on geopolitical interests between states to wars based on identity issues between non-state groups.

Conflict dynamics

While every conflict has different dynamics, analysts have identified similarities between conflicts. Conflicts typically escalate and de-escalate through several phases. Ramsbotham and Woodhouse (1999) formulated a model of conflict dynamics. This helps policymakers to identify the best responses that will help with conflict resolution at each stage of both the escalation and de-escalation of violent conflict.

Stage of conflict	Ideal response	Contemporary examples
Difference	Cultural (or community) peacebuilding	The Southern Sudan Peace Commission was established in 2006 with the objective of promoting peaceful coexistence among the people of South Sudan. It also aimed to develop an early warning system, while trying to build peace between communities.
Contradiction	Structural peacebuilding	After the popular uprisings of the Arab Spring in 2011, Egypt struggled to establish a new order peacefully. There were few political parties to offer the people a democratic choice for the greater representation that many had demanded, particularly minorities. Western governments invested aid money in programmes to build up Egyptian civil society and political parties.

General vocabulary

geopolitical relating to the way that a state's position and population affect its political development and its relationship with other states, or the study of this

dynamics the ways in which things or people behave, react and affect each other

uprisings attempts by a group of people to change the government or laws in an area or state

Synonyms

escalate .... increase in scale

coexistence .... living together

Stage of conflict	Ideal response	Contemporary examples
Polarization	Elite peacemaking	The Israel–Palestine conflict has frequently been focused on peacemaking efforts at elite level. Former British Prime Minister Tony Blair was appointed Special Envoy of the Quartet (US, UN, EU and Russia) on leaving office in 2007, and led elite peacemaking efforts with senior leaders on behalf of the major world powers.
Violence	Peacekeeping	UN peacekeepers were sent to Rwanda in 1994 but their rules of engagement did not allow them to intervene directly to prevent genocide. A major activity of the UN remains peacekeeping. The majority of operations in the last 10 years have been in Africa.
War	War limitation	The African Union Mission to Somalia (AMISOM) was dispatched in 2008 under a UN mandate to conduct peacekeeping operations. By 2012, many analysts agreed that AMISOM has in fact conducted peace enforcement operations in Somalia, fighting against al-Shabaab to regain territory for the interim Somali government.
Ceasefire	Peacekeeping	Colombia's largest left-wing rebel group, the FARC, agreed to a series of ceasefires as it took part in negotiations with the Colombian government between 2012 and 2015.
Agreement	Elite peacemaking	The Good Friday Agreement in Northern Ireland (1998) agrees power sharing between the main political parties in a new Northern Ireland Assembly and the release of political prisoners. The constitution of the Republic of Ireland was amended to revoke the Republic of Ireland's territorial claim to Northern Ireland.
Normalization	Structural peacebuilding	A key part of the peace process in Somalia since 2012 has involved negotiations between the government in the capital, Mogadishu, and regional pro-government clans. Discussions have focused on the sharing of resources and income across the whole of Somalia.
Reconciliation	Cultural (or community) peacebuilding	Truth and Reconciliation Commissions in Sierra Leone (1999) and South Africa (1998). An International Commission of Inquiry on Darfur, Sudan was established by the UN in 2004 and reported in 2005, concluding that the government of Sudan had not pursued a policy of genocide.

Subject vocabulary

elite peacemaking attempts to stop violence which are led by senior leaders, for example prime ministers or presidents

peace enforcement a contested term, where military force is used to bring about an end to violent conflict

Synonyms

revoke .... reverse

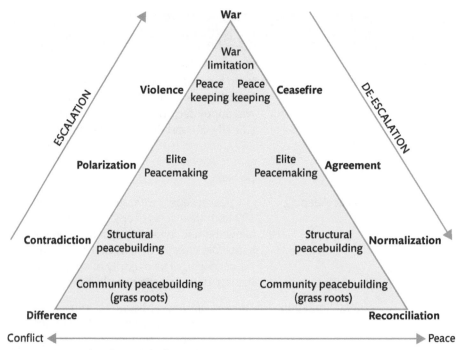

Figure 4.5 *Stages of conflict and conflict resolution*

 Articulation sentence:

Ramsbotham and Woodhouse created a model of conflict dynamics that helps policymakers understand the stages through which conflict escalates and de-escalates, and the ideal responses for resolving conflict at each stage.

4.3 Key concept: Violence and non-violence

Key idea:

Violence is when physical, mental or other harm is caused by an individual or group to another.

Types of violence

Direct violence

Direct violence is when an individual or group is physically or mentally harmed, through direct action. For example, if a bomb attack kills or injures people, then direct violence has taken place. Direct violence also includes crimes against humanity, where **systematic** direct violence is directed at an ethnic group by a group or individual in a position of power. Genocide, as seen in Rwanda in 1994 and in Srebrenica, former Yugoslavia, in 1995, is the most extreme form of direct violence. Genocide is defined by the UN as the attempt to destroy, in whole or in part, a national, ethnic, racial or religious group. In general, direct violence is:

- often straightforward to identify;
- possible to investigate and establish who was responsible;
- possible to measure;
- possible to identify in such a way that those responsible can be **held to account**.

General vocabulary

systematic organized carefully and done thoroughly

Synonyms

held to account ... made or shown to be responsible

Structural violence

Structural violence is when a government or other forms of power functions in a way that results in physical, mental or other harm to individuals or groups. This may be through inequalities that deny people fundamental rights, resulting in physical harm such as illness or death through hunger or disease. A government commits this form of violence when it forcibly and consciously limits human development or undermines well-being, where fairer alternatives are possible.

Violence of any kind must contain some form of intent. A government that is poor and doing its best to provide for all its citizens, but faces a humanitarian disaster beyond its control in which people die, is not guilty of structural violence. By contrast, a government that hoards wealth within an elite, and fails to spend government resources to protect its citizens from preventable diseases, is guilty of structural violence. In general, structural violence:

- is a conscious choice – the structure of government causes physical or mental harm to others;
- leads to preventable suffering not being prevented;
- causes people to be harmed through lack of basic necessities, which may be given to others;
- is widespread, but often unchallenged and unacknowledged;
- is harder to measure and say who is responsible for it.

Cultural violence

Structural violence is very much the responsibility of governments and those in power, but responsibility for cultural violence is embedded within all levels of a society. Cultural violence may be committed in private, in homes and families, as well as in public.

Cultural violence can be identified in the mindset, beliefs and values of a society. For example, in a culture where people believe women are inferior to men and do not deserve the same human rights, there may be higher levels of direct violence against women (such as domestic abuse or honour-based violence at home). Equally, cultural norms that discriminate against women may result in a government failing to protect women and structural violence taking place. In general, cultural violence:

- may be government-driven (culture influencing government structures) or society-driven (grass-roots culture influencing society's behaviour);
- is any aspect of a culture that is used to legitimize violence in its direct or structural forms;
- may be harder to eliminate as it is embedded in the mindset of a society and is linked to cultural or religious values that become seen as legitimate.

> Violence can be direct, structural or cultural. Structural and cultural violence are forms of violence embedded in either the government or culture of a society.

Non-violence

Many political causes are pursued through an active policy of non-violence. The strongest commitment to non-violence is seen in pacifism, which emphasizes peaceful and non-violent solutions to all disputes. Pacifism states that violence and war are unjustifiable in all contexts. Pacifists place considerable importance on developing human rights, the rule of law and strengthening the capacity for international organizations such as the UN to resolve conflict.

CHALLENGE YOURSELF

Thinking, Communication and Social skills

In 2014, Uganda created its Anti-Homosexuality Act (which is now in dispute). Under this law, a person found guilty of committing homosexual acts can be sentenced to life in prison. In groups, discuss whether you think this could be interpreted as structural violence. Does the law deny any fundamental rights and does it cause physical or mental harm?

Synonyms

fundamental .. basic

hoards .... keeps

inferior .... not as important

driven .... strongly influenced

General vocabulary

undermines gradually makes someone or something less strong or effective

well-being a feeling of being comfortable, healthy and happy

embedded put firmly and deeply

mindset someone's general attitude, and the way in which they think about things and make decisions

grass-roots ordinary people, not the leaders

Subject vocabulary

intent the intention to do something illegal

honour-based violence a violent crime or incident which may have been committed to protect or defend the honour of the family or community

pacifism the belief that war and violence are always wrong

It is important to distinguish between groups who use non-violent means and groups who use violent means to achieve a similar final political objective. Islamism, for example, is frequently associated with violent extremism, as seen in Islamic State's violent military campaign to create an Islamic state in Syria and Iraq. However, the objective of a purely Islamic form of government is also pursued non-violently in other contexts. For example, the Muslim Brotherhood set up a political party – the Freedom and Justice Party – and won parliamentary and presidential elections in 2011 and 2012. Some analysts, however, see the potential for non-violent Islamists to progress to violent Islamism and argue that both strongly influence each other. Non-violent causes may, for example, inspire violent acts that others carry out.

 Articulation sentence:
Some states and groups are pacifist and aim to solve conflicts without the use of violence.

Terrorism

Terrorism is a form of violence that has gained significant international attention since the 11 September 2001 attacks on the United States, but it has posed a security risk to nation states for a long time. There is no agreed definition of terrorism. The United Nations has attempted to define it, but as of 2015 had still not reached an agreement. One definition is that terrorism is 'the threat of violence and the use of fear to coerce, persuade and gain public attention' (NACCJSG: 1976).

In order to define a particular group as a terrorist organization, the legitimacy of that group's actions and objectives must be assessed. There is often debate about whether such groups are terrorists or freedom fighters. Different conclusions may be drawn depending on viewpoints, loyalties and victimhood. Such debates centre on a number of questions, including – but not limited to – the following:

- Does the violent group have any non-violent alternatives to violence (for example, a democratic process)?
- Is there a legitimate grievance that makes the threat and use of violence necessary? Morally, is this ever justifiable?
- Are civilians deliberately targeted to create a climate of fear, so that governments will feel obliged to respond?

State terrorism

Nation states that abuse their powers may terrorize their populations through violence and the threat of violence. For example, Saddam Hussein's Ba'ath Party in Iraq attacked Kurdish and Shia minorities with chemical weapons.

Sub-state terrorism

Non-state terrorist groups, such as al-Qaeda and Boko Haram, have carried out attacks against national governments and civilians. In both cases, their operations represent an insurgency which challenged the legitimacy of those in power.

Internationalized terrorism

Since 11 September 2001, terrorist groups have become increasingly globalized. For example, al-Qaeda began to grow into an international network with recruits and activists in many countries, able to carry out terrorist acts across the world. The Paris attacks of November 2015 were seen to be the most significant terrorist act by Islamic State-inspired militants. A key objective of such attacks is to mobilize other militants to carry out similar acts and to terrorize communities through attacks on public places, which attract high-profile international attention.

General vocabulary

coerce force someone to do something they do not want to do by threatening them

Subject vocabulary

freedom fighter someone who fights in a war against an unfair or dishonest government or army

victimhood the state of suffering because someone has treated you very badly

Synonyms

mobilize .... encourage

Articulation sentence:

> Since 11 September 2001, terrorism as a form of violence has been increasing and becoming more globalized.

Justifying violence

While pacifists believe that violence can never be justified, others believe that violence can be both morally and legally justified.

Just war theory

Originating as early as 300 CE, Christian religious thinkers including St Augustine and St Thomas Aquinas attempted to identify criteria by which violence could be justified. Consensus emerged around the following key themes of just war theory.

- Right authority. Those starting violent conflict should have legitimate authority to do so. In modern global politics, nation states have a responsibility to follow international law. In matters of international security, the UN Security Council plays a key role. For example, some question the legality of the Iraq War in 2003 since it was launched without a UN Security Resolution specifically authorizing military action. In contrast, military action against Libya in 2011 was authorized by a UN Security Council Resolution agreeing 'all necessary measures' to protect civilians.

- Just cause. For the cause to be just, it must have the objective of restoring peace. It must not have an objective of material gain, for example of resources or territory. Agreeing on just cause in modern global politics is likely to be a matter of **perspective**.

- Probability of success. If the cause is just, it must also be achievable. Violence in pursuit of an unachievable aim does not comply with the criteria of just war theory.

- Proportionality. Any action taken must be **proportionate** to the initial act of aggression.

- Last resort. Efforts to resolve the conflict peacefully (for example, through diplomacy and negotiation) must have been attempted and been exhausted before violence becomes a legitimate course of action.

Articulation sentences:

> Just war theory governs the decision to begin a conflict. It is a philosophical, not political, consensus. States are not obliged to follow it.

Justifications in international law and norms

- Chapter VII of the United Nations Charter authorizes the UN Security Council to 'determine the existence of any threat to the peace, breach of the peace, or act of aggression' and to take military and non-military action to 'restore international peace and security'. For example, UN Security Council Resolution 1973 authorized a **no-fly zone** and 'all necessary measures' to protect civilians in Libya in 2011. A series of UN Security Council Resolutions invoking Chapter VII of the UN Charter have established and renewed the African Union Mission to Somalia (AMISOM) since 2008.

- Request for help. Military action is seen to be legitimate in international law if a nation state requests help from others. For example, no UN Security Council Resolution was sought for United States-led military action in Iraq against Islamic State in 2014, as Iraq had requested help.

- Responsibility to Protect. In 2005, the UN General Assembly agreed to the principle of states having a 'Responsibility to Protect' their populations from genocide, war crimes, ethnic cleansing and crimes against humanity. If a nation state fails to do so, the UN General Assembly agreed that the international community then has a responsibility to use the powers of the UN Security Council to intervene. However, the principle is not international law. Taking action against states that do not exercise responsible sovereignty depends on the UN Security Council agreeing to take action. The military action launched by NATO against the Gaddafi regime in Libya, in 2011, saw the UN Security Council resolve to 'ensure the protection of civilians'. This is an example of other states committing to protect the civilians of another state from their own government, since Gaddafi had called his citizens 'cockroaches' and 'rats' and threatened them with violence. Some states have invoked the doctrine to justify their own unilateral actions, such as Russian military action in Georgia in 2008.

Jus in bello – conduct during violent conflict

International law and treaties govern the conduct of armed conflict. Agreements by treaty are only binding for states that have signed those treaties and are certainly not binding for non-state groups. Such treaties include:

- Geneva and Hague Conventions – under international humanitarian law, these conventions govern the conduct of armed conflict, including protection of civilians, hospitals, the injured and the proper treatment of prisoners. All member states of the UN are subject to the conventions and the UN Security Council may act in response to any breaches (this is the principle of customary international law, where laws are 'a general practice accepted as law' and exist independent of treaty law. States cannot opt out.)

- The Geneva Protocol – a treaty prohibiting the use of asphyxiating or poisonous gases.

- Ottawa Treaty (1997) – prohibits the use of landmines by treaty.

- Convention on Cluster Munitions (2008) – a treaty applicable in international law only to those states that have signed it, prohibiting the use of cluster bombs.

Articulation sentence:
There are international laws and conventions governing the reasons why a state can enter into a violent conflict as well as how it must behave during the conflict.

Introduction

Objectives of the Higher Level extension

In this part of the course, students must research and deliver two ten-minute oral presentations. They can choose two of six themes in Global Politics, focusing on a specific case study. The presentations are recorded on video. Students are allowed to share one draft of their presentation and discuss it with their teacher, but can only deliver a presentation once for it to be internally assessed. Some presentations from the school will be sent to the International Baccalaureate (IB) for moderating*, just as with other internally assessed work.

The six themes of global political challenges are as follows. Each of these will be explored in greater detail in this chapter.

- Security
- Identity
- Borders
- Environment
- Poverty
- Health

Under each of the themes, major links to key concepts will be explored and linked to some contemporary examples, to help students think of ideas for possible case studies.

Presentation style

It is important to remember that the mark scheme rewards a particular style of presentation. Students should avoid preparing presentations that might be interesting for another audience, but do not meet the mark scheme requirements. Students should keep the syllabus objectives clearly in mind when researching, preparing and delivering presentations.

What must a Higher Level presentation do?

- The presentation must be strongly linked to one of the six themes. If the chosen case study links to identity, the question of identity must be sustained throughout the presentation.
- The research phase is crucial. Students should consult a wide variety of sources, properly acknowledged, and ensure their analysis goes beyond their own instincts or personal viewpoints.
- The case study must be specific enough to be analysed effectively in 10 minutes. In particular, it should not be so broad (for example, 'nuclear disarmament') that deep analysis in the time given would be impossible.
- It is best for the chosen case study to be contemporary but not so current or ongoing that it is impossible to draw longer-term conclusions. As a general guide, case studies that deal with issues that date back at least a year previously work best.
- Under the chosen theme, a case study must be analysed and not merely described. Long explanations of timelines, history and description of current events should be avoided. The mark scheme rewards careful *analysis* of why events happened in the way they did, the wider political, social or economic impact of these events, and the challenges they reveal in relation to the theme chosen.

General vocabulary

draft a piece of writing or a plan that is not yet in its finished form

broad concerning the main ideas or parts of something rather than all the details

Synonyms

sustained ...... continued

ongoing .... continuing to develop

Subject vocabulary

disarmament the process of putting weapons and weapon systems beyond use

* *(from Subject Guide p57) All work submitted to the IB for moderation or assessment must be authenticated by a teacher, and must not include any known instances of suspected or confirmed academic misconduct. Authenticity may be checked by discussion with the student on the content of the work, and scrutiny of one or more of the following.*
  - *The student's initial proposals*
  - *The first draft of the written report for the engagement activity and the written outline of each HL presentation*
  - *The references cited*
  - *The style of writing compared with work known to be that of the student*
  - *The analysis of the written work by a web-based plagiarism detection service*
  - *The style of delivery of the oral presentations compared with delivery known to be characteristic of the student.*

Different political issues must be studied for the requirements of the engagement activity, the HL extension and a potential Extended Essay students may choose to write in global politics. Group engagements may be undertaken by students. However each student must study a different political issue and individually write up his or her own written report. Group work is not permitted for the HL extension.

overarching including or influencing every part of something

overrun take more time or money than intended

persuasive able to make other people believe something or do what you ask

visual aids something such as a map, picture, or film that help people understand, learn, or remember information

slides content displayed on a screen as a visual aid when giving a presentation

autocue a machine that shows the words that someone must say while they are speaking in public, especially on television

stakeholders people or organizations that have an important connection with something, and therefore are affected by its success or failure

- To keep the presentation analytical, it makes sense to pose an **overarching** question at the beginning of the presentation, which is analysed and then answered in the conclusion.
- The presentation should *evaluate* the strengths and weaknesses of various arguments.
- Links should be made to the case study and the wider global political context. Where else, for example, are there similar challenges?
- Presentations should always be balanced and look at an issue from different viewpoints. For example, the views of government and non-government groups or different ethnic or **gender** groups.
- There should be a strong conclusion.
- Presentations must not **overrun**. Teachers and IB moderators will stop marking after ten minutes. It is important to leave enough time for the conclusion, as this will be the last thing to be marked.

Engaging the audience

While presentation skills are not specifically rewarded or penalized in the mark scheme, if a student presents their arguments well, they will be more **persuasive**.

- **Visual aids** are not specifically rewarded in the mark scheme, but may help students to explain more complex concepts. Graphs, maps, tables and charts are the only visual aids permitted. Presentations prepared in PowerPoint or similar are not permitted. **Slides** with bullet-points should not be used, as students will have marks deducted.
- Students should give a clear sense of structure and focus during their presentation. Sign-posting helps. For example, 'This presentation will focus on three key areas – politics, economics and gender. First, politics...'
- Students are allowed to use prompt cards but must not read from a script or **autocue**. The livelier and more enthusiastic the delivery, the better.

Structuring a presentation

Introduction (1–2 minutes)

- The student should state which theme has been chosen, which case study and why the two are linked.
- They should briefly explain the key facts of the case study and which **stakeholders** are involved in it.

Analysis and evaluation – the main part of the presentation (7 minutes)

- What political challenges does the case study raise?
- What links are there to theory or key concepts of the course that can help the analysis?
- How did stakeholders respond and why?
- What were the social, political and economic impacts in this case study?

Conclusion (1–2 minutes)

- How does the case study pose a global political challenge?
- Where else do people face this challenge? What links are there?

5.1 Key theme: Security

Key idea:

Security is the ability to protect against threats to vital **interests** and values.

Most relevant concepts

Interdependence

Interdependence is linked to security because many nation states share the same security threats. For example, nation states have worked together to respond to the threat of global terrorism, particularly since 11 September 2001. Nations often form alliances and work together to protect security interests through international organizations such as NATO and the UN Security Council. States sometimes form informal coalitions of their own, such as the United States-led coalition in Iraq in 2003. States work together on a wide range of **perceived** security threats, ranging from energy security to food and climate security.

Power

Power matters for security, because it is often believed that the most powerful states are the most able to protect their national security. However, recent conflicts during the so-called War on Terror have seen powerful states such as the United States unable to achieve conclusive victories against their enemies. Equally, states with weak internal **sovereignty**, such as **fragile** states, find it difficult to protect their national security. This is illustrated by the **prevalence** of piracy in Somalia. The rise of non-state groups such as Islamic State, Boko Haram and al-Shabaab, together with the increase in **insurgencies** and **asymmetric warfare**, have also challenged beliefs about the ability of powerful states to protect their security.

Legitimacy

Legitimacy is linked to security because illegitimate actions by states or non-state groups frequently pose a security threat. For example, in 2003 the US led a military campaign in Iraq even though it did not have decisive UN Security Council approval. Many people, including the UN Secretary General, Kofi Annan, saw this as a threat to the Security Council and the United Nations' role in maintaining international peace and security. Similarly, **breaches** of international law – such as Russia's **annexation** of Crimea in Ukraine in 2014 – also threaten a rules-based international **order** in which nation states respect each other's internal and external sovereignty.

Sovereignty

Sovereignty plays a key role in discussions about security. Generally speaking, states seek to protect their own national security within their sovereign borders. State security becomes threatened when other states **violate** the sovereignty of others, by both invasion and interference. Responsible sovereignty means that if a state is mistreating its population, other states are allowed and encouraged to intervene. An example of this is Libya in 2011, when NATO air strikes were authorized by the UN Security Council to protect civilians suffering under the corrupt government.

Human rights

Security threats (such as those explained above in relation to responsible sovereignty) and **measures** intended to protect security have an impact on human

General vocabulary

interests the things that bring advantages to someone or something

interdependence a situation in which people or things rely on each other

insurgencies attempts by a group of people to take control of their government using force and violence

legitimacy the fact that something is legal

breaches actions that break a law, rule, or agreement

annexation taking control of a country or area next to your own, especially by using force

order the political, social, or economic situation at a particular time

violate break a law, agreement or principle

Synonyms

perceived ...... believed to be

fragile .... unstable

prevalence .... commonness

measures ...... steps, actions

Subject vocabulary

sovereignty the power that an independent country has to govern itself

asymmetric warfare conflict in which there is an imbalance between the parties, for example in aims, capacity or strategy

rights. Sometimes, human rights are suspended or weakened by governments that want to protect their domestic security. For example, some counter-terrorism measures were introduced after the 11 September 2001 attacks in order to protect domestic security. However, these measures have been criticized on human rights grounds. Prominent domestic examples include the United States' PATRIOT Act, introduced after 11 September 2001, and attempts by the UK Government since 2001 to increase detention without charge for those suspected of terrorist plots. Internationally, the US Government has been criticized for using torture and arbitrary detention at its detention centre at Guantanamo Bay, and for sending suspects to Cuba and elsewhere by extraordinary rendition.

Development

There is a clear relationship between security, and poverty and development. Sometimes, limited human development might create the conditions in which security threats are created and thrive. Equally, a lack of human security – which includes a range of human needs such as food, shelter, employment, healthcare and education – is one of many causes of violent conflict and instability. In recent years, a key part of post-conflict resolution has been improving development, sometimes through ambitious state-building programmes to improve health, education, human rights and infrastructure to avoid a return to conflict.

Peace

Security is enhanced if a community, region or state is at peace. Peacemaking, peacekeeping and peacebuilding are all used to improve security. For example, the African Union peacekeeping force in Somalia has improved internal security and reclaimed territory from the extremist group, al-Shabaab. Similarly, we can analyse the extent to which peacebuilding efforts by intervening forces and development agencies in Afghanistan and Iraq have brought greater security.

Possible case studies

The links to key concepts below are a selection and are not exhaustive.

Case studies	Links to key concepts
African Union Mission to Somalia (AMISOM)	**Peace** – positive or negative? Has AMISOM conducted peacekeeping or peace enforcement operations?
	Development – success of development efforts by UN and Non-governmental Organizations (NGOs).
	Interdependence – regional threat to East Africa and the Indian Ocean. Cooperation between UN Security Council and African Union.
	Sovereignty – strengthening of Somalia's internal sovereignty (Somalia is a fragile state).
US withdrawal from Iraq in 2011	**Power** – why did the US withdraw when it did? Did it do so from a position of strength or weakness? Did the US 'win'?
	Sovereignty – was Iraq stable and strong enough to look after its own security and exercise proper control of its internal sovereignty?
	Peace – what efforts were made to make peace in Iraq? Had enough been done to reconcile Sunni and Shia Muslims?

Case studies	Links to key concepts
US–China tensions in the South China Sea	**Legitimacy/sovereignty** – is China violating international law by building and expanding islands in the South China Sea? **Power** – why is China expanding in the South China Sea? How is the US challenging China? What conclusions can be drawn about the US–China power balance?
Drone strikes in Pakistan between 2008 and 2014	**Sovereignty** – are drone strikes by the US a violation of Pakistani sovereignty? **Human rights/legitimacy** – are drone strikes a justifiable act of war or unjustifiable extrajudicial killings? **Power** – do drone strikes work? Have they reduced the security threat that the US identified? What do they tell us about the strength of the Pakistani government?

Related ideas and debates

Security dilemma and offensive/defensive realism

When states want to increase their national security, they face the possibility that they may **provoke** other states, which may respond by increasing their own security defences. An **arms race** of this kind might threaten the security of both states. The degree of risk depends on whether states are following offensive realism, where states try to gain as much power as possible (as theorized by John Mearsheimer); or defensive realism, where states try to gain only as much power as is necessary and appropriate (as theorized by Kenneth Waltz).

Security alliances and the role of IGOs

For some international organizations, security is their primary objective. The North Atlantic Treaty Organization (NATO) was established during the Cold War. It is a military alliance that offers smaller Western European nations collective security in the face of a threat from the Soviet Union. NATO still exists and has expanded its operations to Afghanistan (2001) and Libya (2011). The prospect of the former Soviet state, Ukraine, joining NATO was one of the factors that prompted the Russian annexation of Crimea in 2014.

The United Nations, through the Security Council, plays a key role in international peace and security. The Security Council can authorize military action, peacekeeping operations, economic **sanctions** and weapons inspections in order to reduce security threats.

Regional organizations, such as the European Union and the **African Union**, have taken an increased interest in security. Since the 2009 Lisbon Treaty, the European Union has a Common Foreign and Security Policy but in reality, the UK and France have taken the lead. The African Union has conducted peace-support operations in Somalia and Sudan, funded by the United Nations.

The War on Terror

Since the 11 September 2001 attacks on the United States, Western powers have focused their security strategies on the global terror threat, principally from Islamist extremist groups such as al-Qaeda. The frequency of terrorist attacks in Western countries has remained relatively stable since 2001, but have increased dramatically in countries where the United States and its allies have launched military action to **counter** terrorism. Iraq, Pakistan, Afghanistan and Nigeria have seen the largest

Subject vocabulary

extrajudicial killings executions carried out by a state or other actor without due legal process

arms race the competition between different countries to have a larger number of powerful weapons

African Union a regional IGO of which most African states are members, focusing primarily on security and economic prosperity

General vocabulary

provoke make someone angry, especially deliberately

sanctions official orders or laws stopping trade or communication with another state, as a way of forcing its leaders to make political changes

counter do something in order to prevent something bad from happening or to reduce its bad effects

Synonyms

taken the lead been most active

increase in terrorist insurgencies since 2001. This raises the question of whether the War on Terror has failed to reduce, and perhaps has even increased, the global terrorist threat.

Other states have increasingly described their own security challenges as a terrorist threat and have used the War on Terror as justification for their own military campaigns. Examples are Russian military action in Chechnya and the Assad regime in Syria's campaign against rebel groups that it calls 'terrorists'.

Nuclear disarmament and non-proliferation

Nuclear security remains a key challenge in the international world order, with disarmament (reduction of current nuclear weapons known to be possessed by states) and non-proliferation (preventing the spread of nuclear weapons to more groups) as the main priorities. The Treaty of the Non-Proliferation of Nuclear Weapons was ratified in 1970, but the global nuclear arsenal is in the region of 20,000 weapons. The number of states possessing nuclear weapons has increased beyond the original countries that signed the treaty (the US, Russia, China, France and the UK) to as many as nine states. These include South Asian rival states, India and Pakistan; and in East Asia, North Korea. Disarmament and non-proliferation have been unsuccessful. Preventing the further spread of nuclear weapons is now focused on the Middle East and curbing the nuclear ambitions of Iran, where a landmark deal was signed in 2015 between Iran and the UN Security Council permanent members and Germany (the so-called P5+1). The risk of nuclear weapons reaching non-state groups is a further threat, to which international organizations remain vigilant.

5.2 Key theme: Identity

Key idea:

Identity is the **distinct** set of characteristics, values, cultures and traditions that distinguish people and groups from others.

Most relevant key concepts

Human rights

Human rights and liberty are fundamentally concerned with the protection of the rights of human beings as individuals, regardless of their identity. For example, the Universal Declaration of Human Rights demands equal protection for human beings regardless of age, race, gender, ethnicity or sexual orientation. Universal human rights can offer protection to minorities who see their human rights challenged, such as when lesbian, gay and transgender (LGBT) people are treated differently purely because of their sexual orientation. However, the concept of universal human rights can sometimes clash with different cultures and values, particularly religious values. States may interpret human rights for some minorities differently, and justify this as 'cultural relativism'. Both governments and communities at grass-roots level can abuse human rights in the name of identity or cultural difference.

Justice

Frequently, the rights of minority groups are either not protected in law, or are actively abused in the codification of the law or in its interpretation by law enforcement agencies such as the police. For example, the rights of women in parts of the Islamic world, notably in Saudi Arabia, are not the same as the rights of men. Equally, laws or customs sometimes explicitly prevent women

Subject vocabulary

non-proliferation preventing the spread of something (often used specifically to refer to nuclear weapons)

global nuclear arsenal total worldwide stock of nuclear weapons

cultural relativism the theory that ideas and other norms should reflect cultural practices and traditions, rather than universal principles

General vocabulary

landmark deal one of the most important deals that influences someone or something

vigilant giving careful attention

distinct clearly different or belonging to a different type

sexual orientation the fact that someone is heterosexual or homosexual

minorities small groups of people or things within a much larger group

clash if two people or groups clash, they argue because they have very different beliefs and opinions - used in news reports

grass-roots ordinary people, not the leaders

codification the arrangement of laws, principles and facts in a system

Synonyms

liberty .... freedom

explicitly .... clearly

CHALLENGE YOURSELF

 Thinking, Communication and Social skills

Saudia Arabia gave women the right to vote in 2015. To what extent do you believe nations should be allowed to preserve their sovereignty? Do you think that states should pressure other states to reform laws that are discriminatory? Discuss your views in groups.

from leading independent and full lives. For example, the Taliban government in Afghanistan before 2001 did not allow girls to attend school or university. In well-developed states, there is criticism that the police treat black and ethnic minority groups differently.

Legitimacy

Legitimacy relates to identity because the identity of individuals and groups is often not recognized by others. Marginalized groups try to gain legitimacy and formal recognition from those in power. For example, indigenous groups in Australia and Canada have received increased recognition in recent years, including apologies from governments who admitted that previous economic and social policies had been unfair.

Sovereignty

Sovereignty offers both the opportunity for identity to be recognized and strengthened, and for identity to be diminished and ignored. For example, Palestinians have long sought international recognition and their own statehood. Gradually they have received greater recognition, including observer status at the United Nations. However, they still do not have full statehood. Within sovereign borders there are often many different ethnic or religious groups that need to be respected and protected. Examples include the Sunni and Shia Muslims in Iraq and Syria, and efforts to build cohesive and integrated communities in states that have large migrant populations, such as the United Kingdom and France.

Denial of identity and the struggle for identity to be respected frequently cause violent and non-violent conflict. For example, the conflict in Northern Ireland between the Protestant and Catholic communities resulted in an armed struggle. Peace processes frequently focus on resolving clashes and disputes of identity, such as the power-sharing agreement between Protestants and Catholics in Northern Ireland in 1998.

Possible case studies

The links to key concepts below are a selection and are not exhaustive.

Case studies	Links to key concepts
Gay marriage in the United States/United Kingdom	**Human rights** – campaigners have argued for equal rights between heterosexual and homosexual couples, focusing on the right to marry.
	Justice – campaigns have led to changes in the law, allowing gay and lesbian couples to marry.
Sunni and Shia conflict in Syria/Iraq	**Sovereignty** – the most prominent Sunni group, Islamic State, has declared a Sunni Islamic caliphate in both Syria and Iraq. It has said that current international borders are irrelevant and it challenges internationally agreed understandings of Iraq and Syria's territory.
	Violence/conflict – a clash between Sunni and Shia is a key cause of conflict; rival militia are organized into Sunni and Shia groups.

General vocabulary

marginalized prevented from having power or influence

migrant someone who goes to live in another area or country, especially in order to find work

caliphate a single Islamic state, uniting many countries with Muslim populations into one much larger state unified by political and religious association with Islam

militia a group of people trained as soldiers, who are not part of the permanent army

Subject vocabulary

indigenous people identified as settled in a place before more recent invasions or migrations

Synonyms

diminished .... reduced

cohesive .... well combined

Case studies	Links to key concepts
Sunni and Shia conflict in Syria/Iraq	**Power** – pro-Shia governments, notably in Iraq, have been accused of neglecting the needs of the Sunni community. In Iraq, there has been a shift in power between Sunni (under President Saddam Hussein and the Ba'ath Party) and Shia (under Prime Minister Nouri al-Maliki). This power struggle is reflected in the regional powers that have taken sides in the conflict, notably Shia Iran and Sunni Saudi Arabia.
Kurdish separatism in Turkey, Iraq and Syria; the Kurdistan Worker's Party (PKK)	**Sovereignty** – many Kurds in Syria, Iraq and southern Turkey believe they should have their own Kurdish state. Kurds have been granted greater autonomy in Iraqi Kurdistan since 2007. **Legitimacy** – demands for an autonomous Kurdish state would change the existing borders of Iraq, Turkey, Syria and possibly Iran. Is there a legitimate claim for a Kurdish state based on how Kurds are treated by the states in which Kurds currently live?
Women's rights in Saudi Arabia and Sharia law	**Justice** and **legitimacy** – the law of Saudi Arabia is based on Sharia law interpreted by the Senior Council of Scholars, the highest state body ruling on Islamic law. **Human rights** – independent NGOs criticize Saudi Arabia for retaining a male guardianship system which ignores the rights of women.

Related ideas and debates

A clash of civilizations

Academic Samuel P Huntington's 1996 essay, 'The Clash of Civilisations', predicted that the main future cause of conflict would be clashes of cultural identity rather than political ideology. Many suggest that Huntington's prediction has been proven right, given the conflict between violent Islamism and Western powers since 2001. However, it is important to note the successful coexistence of a majority of moderate Muslims with Western culture and values at global, regional and national levels.

Religious identity

Some analysts suggest that the importance of religious identity is increasing in global politics. Certainly, there has been an increase in the influence of fundamentalist religious groups such as Boko Haram, al-Shabaab, al-Qaeda and Islamic State, which support a violent extremist interpretation of Islam. In Western Europe, some countries disagree on how best to accommodate religious difference within societies. Two key approaches include secularism (where religion should not intrude into non-religious activities, notably education) and multiculturalism (where religious and other cultural diversity should be actively celebrated, even accommodated in non-religious activities, such as through faith schools).

Feminism and gender identity

Feminism involves greater attention to women's experiences in any analysis of foreign, social or economic policy. It is a question of focus and perspective. Analysts have noticed structural violence towards women where governments treat women differently to men, excluding women from basic rights and services. Looking at key situations in global politics from a feminist perspective might include analysing the impact of conflict on women. Examples include the treatment of women under Taliban rule and the consequent insurgency in Afghanistan; or the impact of economic sanctions in Iran or Iraq on women as opposed to men.

Nationalism

Nationalism has caused major conflict in history and continues to be both a destabilizing and stabilizing force in global politics. Some analysts suggest that globalization, particularly the erosion of national identity through cultural globalization, has increased nationalist tendencies. In Western Europe, there has been a rise in popularity of nationalist parties such as France's Front National and the United Kingdom Independence Party. There have been separatist movements in Catalunya in Spain, and Scotland voted by a small margin to remain part of the United Kingdom in a 2014 referendum.

Nationalism has also played an important role in the Middle East. Strong, autocratic nationalist leaders such as Hosni Mubarak, Bashar al-Assad and Muammar Gaddafi suppressed ethnic tensions and kept ethnically and religiously divided states such as Egypt, Syria and Libya largely united. Since the Arab Uprisings, ethnic and religious conflict has increased in states where there are no longer strong, nationalist leaders.

5.3 Key theme: Borders

Key idea:

Borders are the internationally agreed boundaries between nation states and are central to the concepts of internal sovereignty and external sovereignty.

Most relevant concepts

Sovereignty

Sovereignty is inextricably linked to the concept of borders. A state's internal sovereignty is defined by its territorial borders. The Treaty of Westphalia (also known as the Peace of Westphalia) in 1648 contained the first modern conception of the nation state. The post-Westphalian global order agrees borders internationally and respects the borders of other states. Nation states usually have control over what happens within their borders and respect the borders of other states by not interfering in their affairs. External sovereignty allows states to be recognized on the global stage and to have independent relationships with other states.

Interdependence

Interdependence suggests that, while borders still exist, their importance is decreasing in an increasingly globalized world. Shared challenges such as migration, terrorism, climate change and opportunities such as trade mean that nation states depend on each other. What happens in one state can affect other states. For example, the global financial crisis of 2008 began with a financial crash in the

United States, but had a much larger impact across Europe and beyond. In Europe, borders have all but disappeared and there is free movement of people and goods across the European Union's free trade area. Member states recognize that removing territorial barriers is beneficial for all member states.

Human rights

Human rights have links to borders. Firstly, borders are irrelevant because universal human rights apply to all individuals. Being entitled to human rights is not dependent on where people live. There are also specific human rights that protect migrants: the right to seek asylum if a person is in danger in their home country, the right to freedom of movement, protection from human trafficking and the right to nationality.

Conflict

Conflict often happens when there is a dispute about borders. For example, the borders between India and Pakistan in the region of Kashmir have been disputed and fought over since the late 1940s. The borders between Israel and Palestine are also in dispute, with UN Security Council resolutions still requiring Israel to retreat from territory seized in the 1960s. Non-state terrorist groups such as Boko Haram, Islamic State and al-Shabaab have directly challenged the internationally recognized borders of states. They have seized territory and even declared a new Islamic State stretching across the border of Iraq and Syria.

Peace

Peace processes and international organizations often try to resolve disputes between states that disagree over international borders. The International Court of Justice (ICJ) decides on states' territorial waters. It has also resolved border disputes and claims to sovereignty by states, including Kosovo's claim to independence in 2008, which was rejected by the ICJ. China has refused to recognize the ICJ's rulings and authority in disputes over territorial waters in the South China Sea.

Possible case studies

The links to key concepts below are a selection and are not exhaustive.

Case studies	Links to key concepts
European Union Schengen Agreement Accession of Eastern European member states in 2008 European migrant crisis in 2014–16	**Sovereignty** and **power** – what is the impact of EU membership on member states' sovereignty? Critics of the EU say that member states no longer have the power to control their own borders. **Interdependence** – how effectively does the European Union control its internal and external borders? How well do EU member states work together on common security threats? The migrant crisis of 2014–16 showed a lack of agreement between EU member states on how many migrants to accept from the Middle East. France briefly closed its borders after the Paris terror attacks in 2015. What were the implications for the idea of an internally borderless European Union?

Case studies	Links to key concepts
India and Pakistan dispute over Kashmir	**Sovereignty** and **legitimacy** – the borders between India and Pakistan in the region of Kashmir are disputed. Both India and Pakistan claim sovereignty over Kashmir.
	Peace and **violence** – in the absence of a peace agreement, the border regions have been monitored by one of the United Nations' longest peacekeeping operations. There are frequent clashes between the Indian and Pakistani militaries and militant groups from both sides. The fact that both states possess nuclear weapons adds a further dangerous **dynamic** to the conflict. Attempts by third parties to resolve the conflict have been rejected by India.
Afghanistan–Pakistan border in the War on Terror	**Power** – the border regions between Pakistan and Afghanistan are not under the control of either Pakistan or Afghanistan.
	Sovereignty – the United States has increased drone strikes in Pakistan. Does this amount to a **violation** of Pakistan's sovereignty?
Israeli security fence	**Legitimacy** – the security fence was constructed in territory that UN Security Council resolutions have said Israel should withdraw from. Israel defends the legitimacy of the security fence, saying that it is needed to prevent terrorist attacks from Palestinian groups.
	Power – critics of Israel say that it has been allowed not only to ignore UN Security Council resolutions, but to construct a new border against international law. The UN Security Council has been unable to issue further resolutions as the United States has **vetoed** many UN Security Council resolutions critical of Israel.

General vocabulary

dynamic the way in which things or people behave, react and affect each other

violation an action that breaks a law, agreement or principle

vetoed refused to allow something to happen, by having the right to special powers which allow an actor to legitimately stop what other actors want

porous easy to pass through or get into something

Related ideas and debates

Crossing borders

An increasingly dominant feature of modern global politics has been that borders are more **porous** to both people and issues of common concern. Conflicts in the Middle East and North Africa since the Arab Uprisings have caused large numbers of migrants to attempt to cross the Mediterranean Sea and reach the European Union to claim asylum. European Union states have been unsure about the solution. Is it better to prevent migrants from fleeing conflict zones by attempting to resolve conflicts and address humanitarian crises at the source? Or is it better to welcome migrants, particularly highly skilled migrants who might contribute positively to the receiving country's economy?

Borders are also crossed and exploited by non-state groups, both violent extremist groups and organized criminal groups smuggling drugs or weapons.

Furthermore borders offer no protection from shared challenges such as climate change and **pandemic** disease.

Subject vocabulary

pandemic disease that affects people over a very large area or the whole world

Protecting borders

Despite the increasingly porous nature of borders, states still make great efforts to protect their borders. The Mexico–United States barrier was built to protect against illegal migration from Mexico to the United States. The United Kingdom has chosen to keep its border checks and has opted out of the Schengen Agreement (most other European Union states no longer require internal checks within the European Union). The security fence between Israel and Palestine has been justified by Israel as protection against terrorist attacks, but has been widely criticized. The border between Gaza and Egypt is heavily protected. The Egyptian government has constructed an underground barrier to prevent militants from building tunnels to smuggle weapons into Gaza.

Liberalizing/breaking down borders

As world trade has increased, the significance of international borders has decreased. It is positive for states if it is easy for companies, people and goods to move around the world free from excessive regulation. The most significant example of this has been the creation of the European Union free trade area, with a single currency in most member states and full freedom of movement of people and goods. The Trans-Pacific Partnership agreement, signed between the United States and major economic powers of the Pacific Rim (not including China), has agreed to remove many tariff barriers between states, effectively reducing the importance of borders to trade in the region.

Agreeing borders

The international order offers considerable clarity in deciding and agreeing borders. The United Nations Security Council and the International Court of Justice both play a major role in confirming the legitimacy of state borders. Many new states have been created in the post-colonial period since the 1960s. Some new states have been created very recently, such as South Sudan in 2011. The post-conflict reconstruction of the former Yugoslavia under the Dayton Peace Accords in 1995 saw many new states formed – most recently, Montenegro became an independent state in 2006. Kosovo's parliament declared independence in 2008, but this has yet to be fully recognized by the United Nations, though Kosovo is an independent member of other IGOs such as the International Monetary Fund.

However, in some parts of the world borders have yet to be agreed. The borders between Israel and Palestine remain disputed in the Gaza Strip, the West Bank and the Golan Heights. Between India and Pakistan in Kashmir there is an ongoing border dispute. The sovereignty of Taiwan is disputed between Taiwan and the People's Republic of China. Many of these territorial disputes remain in stalemate.

Subject vocabulary

tariff a tax on goods coming into or going out of a country

General vocabulary

stalemate a situation in which it seems impossible to settle an argument or disagreement, and neither side can get an advantage

CHALLENGE YOURSELF

 Research and Self-management skills

Borders could be linked to interdependence through the issue of climate change. Research the 2015 Paris climate conference. Write a list of possible topics you could cover in a presentation on borders and interdependence.

5.4 Key theme: Environment

Key idea:

The environment relates to the natural world, including air, water, land, animals, plants and resources that states share responsibility for managing, without inflicting harm for current or future generations.

Most relevant concepts

Globalization

Globalization impacts on environmental political issues: since the world has become more globalized and industrialized, there has been increased scope for harm to be done to the environment. There have been many more global actors involved in activities that might harm the environment, ranging from multinational corporations to states.

Interdependence

Interdependence means that environmental problems will usually impact on more than one state. For example, rising temperatures and climate change impact on many, rather than single, states. Most meaningful solutions to environmental problems must therefore also be tackled by states together, rather than in isolation, as joint solutions are the only ones likely to achieve the necessary impact. For example, international conferences such as the Copenhagen and Paris talks on climate change have seen states come together to find ways of reducing the impact of climate change.

Synonyms

tackled .... dealt with

Sustainability

Sustainability involves ensuring that meeting the development needs of today does not put the development needs of tomorrow at risk. The new Sustainable Development Goals replaced the Millennium Development Goals in 2015 and there is now increased global agreement that development must follow a sustainable model.

Sovereignty and conflict

Sovereignty and conflict are linked to the environment, for example, in relation to energy security which is likely to impact on potential future conflicts. The Arctic Circle is a good example, where Russia is using its military power to increase its presence and sovereign claim to valuable potential sources of oil. States have also responded to international proposals to combat climate change by defending their sovereign right to protect their national industries from international limits on emissions that might harm their development.

CHALLENGE YOURSELF

Research and Self-management skills

Find out what the Millennium Development Goals were from the UN website. Now find the new Sustainable Development Goals. What has changed between them and what has stayed the same? Make a table of your findings.

Possible case studies

The links to key concepts below are a selection and are not exhaustive.

Case studies	Links to key concepts
Recent climate change talks (for example, Copenhagen 2009, Paris 2015)	**Globalization** – has globalization made international agreements easier or more difficult to achieve? **Interdependence** – is there a consensus that states share common problems as a result of climate change? Or do states share a common problem (climate change) that manifests itself in different ways to different states? Do rich and poor states not face completely different dangers arising from climate change, with a greatly differing sense of urgency? **Power** – what is the balance of power between developed nations (the United States), emerging developing nations (Brazil, China and India) and developing nations (such as those in sub-Saharan Africa)?
BP Gulf of Mexico oil spill 2010	**Power** – what does the case study tell us about the balance of power between large multinational corporations and state systems of government? **Interdependence** – how well did states in the region coordinate on the aftermath of the oil spill? Did IGOs play a useful role in managing the aftermath or were other actors more relevant? What was the impact on UK and US relations? **Justice** – is international law strong enough in holding BP accountable for its actions?
Airport expansion (for example, the current debate around Heathrow expansion in the UK)	**Legitimacy** – how are decisions made on major infrastructure projects that will impact on the environment? **Power** – which actors hold power over major infrastructure decisions like these? Do multinational corporations and businesses hold more power than local residents who will be affected most directly by these projects?

Related ideas and debates

The global commons

The phrase 'global commons' relates to environmental resources that are shared by states and that do not come under the single sovereign jurisdiction of one nation state. For example, oceans and the ocean floor in international waters are not owned by one nation state and therefore the international community has a shared responsibility for managing and protecting them from harm. Similarly, the cleanliness or pollution of the earth's upper atmosphere is an issue of joint responsibility for nations to protect. The phrase 'tragedy of the commons' relates to the idea of a conflict of interest between individual and collective interest, with the former potentially putting the environment under increasing pressure.

Free riders

On environmental issues, 'free riders' are actors in global politics that opt out of collective agreements to prevent harm to the environment (such as emissions targets aimed at limiting climate change). However, they still take advantage of the benefits created by those who do commit to such collective agreements.

Balance of responsibility between rich and poor countries

A key debate in recent climate change talks has been balancing the prevention of harm to the environment and not impeding the development of states. Developed states such as the United States have been criticized for demanding that developing states adopt emissions targets that might impede their economic development. Such states are encouraged to invest in renewable energy, but argue that developed states were not impeded by the need to respect the environment when they were at equivalent levels of economic development.

Synonyms	
impeding	preventing
impede	prevent

Climate change and natural disasters

The Intergovernmental Panel on Climate Change (IPCC) is an independent body of scientists, appointed by nation states, to advise the UN on the science and extent of climate change. The IPCC has helped inform nation states and can be credited with the consensus that now exists among developed and developing states of the existence of man-made change and the need to combat it. There is global consensus now, too, that natural disasters (such as hurricanes and flooding) have been influenced by climate change, are becoming more frequent and more serious and that sea levels are rising.

5.5 Key theme: Poverty

Key idea:

Poverty is to be deprived of basic human needs that are vital for life, such as food, shelter, fuel and clothing. It may be either 'absolute' if human survival is under immediate threat, or 'relative' if compared with the wealth or needs enjoyed by others.

Most relevant concepts

Development

Development is relevant because it is seen to include the key activities and policies aimed at reducing poverty. Many measures of development focus on measuring poverty, either absolute or relative poverty. The Millennium Development Goals included reducing poverty as a key objective from 2000 to 2015, and this objective has been retained in their successor, the Sustainable Development Goals. Many different types of development – ranging from economic development to human development – have reducing poverty as their aim.

Globalization and inequality

Globalization and inequality are relevant to poverty, particularly with regard to the debate as to whether globalization has reduced or increased global inequality. Economic progress in developing states such as China and India have succeeded in reducing the global gap between rich and poor, but in other parts of the world – notably sub-Saharan Africa – the gap between rich and poor has been widening. There is also a debate as to whether multinational corporations take advantage of developing states or whether they empower them and help developing states with their economic and human development. Inequality also exists within states, with many states seeing an increase in the gap between rich and poor.

Justice

Justice has often been cited as a key part of reducing poverty, with worldwide campaigns often framed in terms of delivering justice to those in poverty. There have been national campaigns based around the notion of 'social justice', connected to ideas of fair pay, provision of welfare payments and tax relief to support those on lower incomes. Political parties across the political spectrum are interested in ideas of social justice, but differ on how it can be achieved. At a global level, there have been debates about debt cancellation and debt relief for poor countries, often linked to notions of justice between rich and poor countries.

Conflict and violence

Conflict and violence are frequently identified as drivers of poverty. Structural violence will result in poverty if the state actively chooses policies that deny basic human needs to certain groups. Direct violence also causes poverty by causing injury or destroying the infrastructure through which the basic human needs of a population are delivered, such as food, shelter, schools or hospitals. Countries in conflict are more likely to experience deeper levels of human poverty than countries that are at peace. Poverty is 20 per cent higher in countries experiencing conflict. The displacement of populations and refugees in conflict regions further contributes to worsening poverty.

Possible case studies

The links to key concepts below are a selection and are not exhaustive.

Case studies	Links to key concepts
Make Poverty History campaign and Gleneagles G8 Summit 2005	**Power** – how powerful are social movements that pressure governments to reduce poverty? Why was this protest movement powerful? Did governments respond adequately to the demands of the protest movement? Did powerful states look to preserve their economic power or did they try to balance power to alleviate poverty in poorer countries?
	Justice – were the demands of Make Poverty History fair and focused on delivering justice? Is debt relief and debt cancellation one way of ensuring greater justice between rich and poor countries?
	Development – were the goals of debt relief and debt cancellation sensible for reducing poverty? Does an increase in aid help reduce poverty?
The Millennium Development Goals (MDGs)	**Development** – were the MDGs successful in reducing poverty? In which regions were the MDGs most and least successful? What is the value of globally agreed targets like the MDGs?
(perhaps choosing a particular region or country to focus on)	**Equality** – have the MDGs reduced inequality? How can states break down the inequalities of income and of gender? Has the gap between rich and poor been reduced?
	Conflict – the MDGs did not mention conflict prevention as a key target. Some were critical of this. The Sustainable Development Goals do not mention conflict prevention either. Is this a sensible approach?

Case studies	Links to key concepts
Horn of Africa famine 2011	**Development** – what were the principal causes of the famine? The region suffered from extreme poverty, so what was the relationship between this pre-existing poverty and the famine?
	Conflict – the Horn of Africa region suffers from a long-standing civil war. What impact did this have on the famine? Did it make the famine more likely to happen? Did it make the famine more devastating and difficult to resolve once it had happened?

Related ideas and debates

The Washington Consensus

The Washington Consensus sets out a series of neoliberal economic policies that were agreed in the late 1980s as the best economic model for states' development. They focus on keeping public spending and taxes low, maintaining free trade, privatizing state-owned corporations and keeping regulation on financial markets low. These ideas have frequently been used by economic IGOs such as the International Monetary Fund as a way of bargaining with countries that receive aid to produce wider outcomes in line with the neoliberal model.

Absolute poverty

Absolute poverty is defined as the absence of basic needs. Developed states such as the United States, Canada and Western European states would have very low, perhaps non-existent, levels of absolute poverty. The United Nations defines absolute poverty as living on less than $1.90 per day. Middle- and high-income countries can choose their own absolute poverty line.

Relative poverty

Relative poverty is defined as the poverty experienced by one individual or group in comparison with another. This is more likely to exist in developed nations, where the gap between rich and poor may be particularly acute. Relative poverty focuses on those who are less wealthy but not in an urgent state of deprivation of basic human needs. Relative poverty is defined in relation to the overall distribution of income in a country. This measure is most useful for measuring poverty in middle- and high-income countries.

Poverty cycle

The poverty cycle refers to the idea that poor countries become trapped in a state of poverty. For example, some of the least progress towards the Millennium Development Goal to reduce poverty has been seen in sub-Saharan Africa. A combination of factors that impede development – such as disease, poor governance, conflict and corruption – work together to exacerbate conditions of absolute poverty. These factors hold back economic, social, political and human development, working against many of the key types of development seen in Unit 3 (pages 48–63).

Synonyms

famine	extreme food shortage
acute	severe
overall	general
trapped	caught
least	smallest

General vocabulary

civil war a war in which opposing groups of people from the same country fight each other in order to gain political control

governance the act of making all the decisions about taxes, laws and public services

corruption dishonest, illegal or immoral behaviour, especially from someone with power

CHALLENGE YOURSELF

Research, Thinking and Self-management skills

In 2013, author Thomas Piketty published his book *Capital in the Twenty-First Century*. In it he proposed a new method for redistributing wealth between the rich and the poor. Research on the internet what his proposal was and read an excerpt of the book if possible. Do you think his ideas are helpful and achievable?

Global inequality

Global inequality refers to the idea that there is a gap between the rich and poor countries of the world and that it has been widening over recent years. A recent Oxfam campaign has highlighted that the combined wealth of the richest 1 per cent will overtake that of the other 99 per cent in the next few years unless action is taken to reduce the current trends of rising inequality. Global campaigners would like to see action taken to introduce minimum wages for all workers, a minimum income guarantee and sharing the tax burden more fairly from taxing labour to taxing capital and wealth.

5.6 Key theme: Health

Key idea:

Health in global politics refers to the ability of actors in global politics to manage risks to public health at national, regional and international level, ranging from global pandemics to national outbreaks of disease and prevention of ill health.

Most relevant concepts

Globalization and interdependence

With increased globalization and movement of people across borders, there has been increased risk of the spread of global pandemic diseases. Recent years have seen the Ebola outbreak across West Africa, threatening countries far beyond that region and demanding an international response.

Human rights and justice

Human rights and justice relate directly to the access of resources for adequate healthcare. Equally, there are important human rights debates surrounding health, the right to life and the right to access adequate standards of healthcare.

Development

Development is a central theme as access to and the inadequate provision of healthcare can result in significant health-related inequalities. Examples range from the debates over Obamacare in the US to child mortality and maternal health, which was a key focus of the Millennium Development Goals.

Violence

Violence plays a part through the notion of structural violence and through the impact that violent conflict has on health, security and prevention of disease.

Possible case studies

The links to key concepts below are a selection and are not exhaustive.

Case studies	Links to key concepts
Ebola outbreak 2014–15	**Globalization** – how did the outbreak spread? What were the key elements of globalization that contributed to the spread of Ebola? How did political globalization, the increased cooperation between nation states, help to resolve the outbreak? **Development** – what impact did development issues or deficiencies in affected countries have on the spread of the outbreak?
Decline of HIV/AIDS in Brazil or China	**Sovereignty** – how have states used their internal sovereignty to tackle the spread of HIV/AIDS? Which policies have been particularly successful? **Development** – how have these states approached tackling HIV/AIDS in terms of development policy and priorities?
Tackling obesity with state policy (e.g. UK sugar tax, 2016)	**Sovereignty** and **legitimacy** – is it the moral and political duty of the state to reduce obesity among its citizens? What are the economic pressures put on public services by health problems such as obesity?

Synonyms

spread .... extend

deficiencies ... weaknesses

General vocabulary

obesity a term used to describe someone who is very overweight, with a lot of body fat

avian flu an infectious type of influenza that spreads amongst birds

Related ideas and debates

Global pandemics

Pandemics represent a critical threat to human security across the world. Recent outbreaks such as the Ebola virus (2014–15) and the avian flu outbreak (2004–05) caused major global concern and were responded to by states and by health IGOs such as the World Health Organization.

State provision of healthcare

State healthcare remains a key part of the economic and social rights that states have a duty to provide for their citizens. There is, however, a wide range of state healthcare provision, from free-at-the-point-of-use healthcare to all citizens (such as the United Kingdom's National Health Service) and state health insurance schemes (such as the United States' Obamacare). With many Western states facing ageing populations, there is a key debate around the sustainability of public healthcare systems and the best ways of funding and prioritizing state healthcare.

A key component of the Global Politics course is the engagement activity, where students actively investigate a political issue of their choice and then write an analytical report exploring the issue they have chosen.

Students do this by organizing a project that allows them to research and experience a political issue first-hand. This is followed by writing a 2,000-word report which combines the research, the activity and the analysis of the chosen political issue.

The engagement activity is one of the many aspects of the Global Politics coursework that differentiates it from more traditional courses in social sciences. The coursework activities are intended to allow students to explore and to reflect on the ways in which politics has an influence on, and is influenced by, people at local, regional or global levels.

This section of the book describes the requirements for the engagement activity and offers some practical advice towards completing this essential part of the course. The engagement activity is worth 25 per cent of the overall marks at Standard Level and 20 per cent at Higher Level.

What is the engagement activity?

The engagement activity is an essential component of the IB Global Politics course. At its core, this project offers students the opportunity to:

- develop in-depth knowledge about a particular topic or subject;
- apply knowledge and theory gained in the classroom by talking to fellow students and professionals;
- receive positive social support from colleagues, professionals, and the teacher throughout the process;
- connect their learning to the world beyond the classroom.

Students need to write a 2,000-word report which shows:

- analysis of a political issue;
- exploration and direct investigation of the chosen issue through an activity they have organized.

The engagement activity tests and develops a number of key skills. Each of these can be thought of as separate stages or tasks to complete:

1 Identifying a political issue of interest and planning an effective and suitable activity that will allow the political issue to be properly analysed.

2 Researching a political issue through active engagement. Organizing, making sense of, and synthesizing evidence gained through the primary activity and secondary research.

3 Writing a report which investigates the political issue and binds together information gained through the student's own activity with secondary research.

Stage 1 – Identifying the issue and the activity

This is a crucial part of the process and sufficient time should be devoted to choosing both the political issue and the activity.

It is recommended that students first choose the political issue, then look for an activity or activities that will allow them to explore the issue properly. The combination of a suitable political issue and an appropriate activity then allow the student to pose a research question that they will realistically be able to actively investigate and analyse.

POLITICAL ISSUE + ACTIVITY ⟶ RESEARCH QUESTION

Students should remember the following when choosing their political issue.

- **Will it be possible to organize an activity that allows the student to explore the political issue?**
  For example, a student may be interested in Russian air strikes in Syria, but is unlikely to be able to investigate this through their own activity. Instead, local and national issues, close to the student's own community or home country, may be more suitable than choosing issues that are currently grabbing international headlines. For example, issues such as the representation of women in the national politics of the student's home country or the local politics involved in a controversial local infrastructure project are likely to allow the student to get much closer to the actors and politics than, for example, Russian air strikes in Syria.

- **Is the political issue of sufficient depth to allow political analysis?**
  It is recommended that the student chooses a political issue first. Some students have been driven towards their political issue because they already have an activity ready and waiting. They then attempted to create a political issue out of an activity that, although praiseworthy, is not very political. For example, choosing volunteering in a beach clean-up as the activity and then writing about the politics of volunteering or beach cleaning is unlikely to raise really deep political issues that the student could analyse in their report.

- **Will the chosen political issue be of interest to the student?**
  Given the freedom to choose any political issue, students should of course choose something of interest to them.

A good test of a political issue is that it should have the right balance between:

Accessibility – can the student actually gain access to, and experience, the political issue directly? Is this possible geographically? Is the activity safe?

Political content – is there enough in the issue to analyse? Are there links with the key concepts and learning outcomes of the course?

Once the political issue has been chosen, the student must then plan an activity or activities that will allow them to explore the issue.

Students should remember the following when planning activities.

- **Research question.** It often helps to develop the political issue into a research question that the activity will allow the student to explore.

Example 1
If the political issue chosen is 'major rail infrastructure projects in the UK', the student could develop this issue into a research question supported by the activity or activities, such as 'How effectively is the public consulted about a major rail infrastructure project in the UK?' The activity is then designed to include the student interviewing a range of political actors involved in the process (for example, a local member of parliament representing their constituents' views; the views of local residents; the views of the business community; the views of the rail company building the project).

- **Multiple perspectives.** The best activities will see students engage with different opinions and viewpoints, so that they can compare these and test the validity of opposing views.

Example 2

If the political issue is the representation of women in politics, it will be important to gain access to the views of both men and women on the obstacles and possible solutions. Students should therefore avoid interviewing a single source, for the same reasons given in Example 1.

- **Design.** Activities must be designed to support investigating a specific political issue, not the other way round. Some students rely on an activity that has perhaps been organized for another purpose, such as work experience in business or volunteering in a school. The students then find it difficult to build a really strong link between the activity and the political issue. The best activities will be designed with the specific political issue in mind.

- **Organization.** Designing the best engagement activity is likely to take time. A key test for students will be contacting a range of political actors and setting up activities or appointments, finding public events to attend, etc. Some students may have high-level contacts in politics or business that they may wish to use, but these are not necessary for an activity to be successful. In fact, some of the best activities are those that interact not with senior politicians but grass-roots activists or communities affected by bigger political decisions. It is recommended that teachers and students begin this process early in the first year of study. The activities can be carried out during the holiday period between the first and second years of study. The report is then written in the early part of the second year of study.

- **Simulation activities.** These can be very good, but there is a risk that activities such as Model United Nations (MUN) or other simulations become too theoretical and distant from real-life events. It is also the case that if students are doing the same engagement activity as others in their class, each student should study a different research question, or provide their own angle on the question. This is harder to do in MUN-style activities. Students should, wherever possible, root themselves in analysing how politics really works. Combining a simulation exercise with an activity that allows the student to explore the issue through real-world events is better than a simulation exercise alone (for example, visiting a refugee charity to explore its work and then carrying out a simulation exercise which explores the difficult choices experienced by the political actors involved).

Stage 1 activities

Political issue and research question	Good activity	Less good activity
Representation of women in UK politics 'Why are women under-represented in elected political office in the UK?'	The student has no links with any female MPs but writes to their local council and meets female councillors, interviewing a variety of actors about their experiences, the challenges they have faced.	The student has links with one female MP and chooses to interview this MP about her experiences. No other activity organized.

Political issue and research question	Good activity	Less good activity
	The student might then organize any of the following:	
	To attend a panel discussion on female representation in politics.	
	To interview aspiring female politicians from a university politics society.	
	To interview male councillors comparing their experiences.	
	To conduct secondary desk-top research on the barriers faced by women in politics.	
The refugee crisis in Europe 'What are the challenges faced by a national NGO in responding to the European refugee crisis?'	The student takes part in a role play activity, playing the role of an NGO trying to lobby EU governments to take more action. The student might then organize any of the following: To visit a national NGO involved in the refugee crisis and interview grass-roots activists on the challenges they face. To conduct an online interview with a more senior representative from the NGO. To attend a panel discussion where NGOs debate the challenges they face.	The student takes part in a role play activity, playing the role of an NGO trying to lobby EU governments to take more action. No other activity organized.

Subject vocabulary

lobby try to persuade the government or someone with political power that a law or situation should be changed

Stage 2 – Carrying out the activity

Students should remember the following when carrying out activities.

- **Keep the research question in mind.** There is a risk that when the activity begins, it becomes driven by the people or groups that the student is meeting or working with. It is worth the student being clear with those they are meeting, working or volunteering with, what it is that they are trying to get out of the activity. This does not mean that they will not be able to offer something in return. But it is not uncommon for students to carry out work experience where the original point of the activity (researching a political issue) becomes side-lined.

- **Effective note-taking.** Students should be organized with their note-taking so they have a clear record of the activity when they come to write about the activity. The notes from interviews need to be included as appendices to the report. Students should seek permission from those they are working with before recording interviews.

General vocabulary

side-lined given lesser priority than other content

- **Gaps where secondary research is needed.** As students carry out the activity, it is worth noting where the activity has raised questions that need further investigation. Are there different perspectives that need to be examined? Could any of these be explored with another, smaller-scale activity, perhaps with another contact recommended by the organization or individual that the student has been working with?

- **Links to the prescribed content and key concepts.** A key skill in writing the report is to make connections between the activity and the key concepts of the course (for example, power, sovereignty, development, human rights, etc.). This is assessed in the markscheme as the student effectively 'synthesizing' their material. Students should keep notes on how the experience relates to the key concepts and learning outcomes of the course.

Stage 3 – Writing the report

Before considering in detail how to write the report, it is worth drawing attention to the two most common mistakes that students make when presenting the first draft of their reports.

Report is dominated by the activity, with no analysis	Report forgets about the activity, with or without analysis
• The student writes only about the activity and does so in narrative, rather than analysis.	• The student writes only about the political issue, perhaps analysing it, but more in the style of an Extended Essay.
• The report reads like an account of who they met, what they did, what they saw, what they were told, how they felt about what they saw and heard.	• There is no link between the activity and the issue, it feels as if the student has focused more on secondary research.
• There is little analysis of what their experiences tell us about the political issue or how it links to and helps us understand the key concepts or learning outcomes of the course.	• There is a sense that the activity was of little importance or relevance to the political issue, which is why the student rarely mentions the activity.

The simplest advice is that reports should be a balance between these two extremes, aiming to clearly ***demonstrate how the activity has helped build an analytical understanding of a political issue***.

The engagement activity is assessed against a markscheme, as is the case with every piece of coursework that students submit for assessment in IB courses. For the engagement activity, the markscheme is divided into four sections. The report is marked out of 20, as follows.

Assessment criteria for the written report

Criterion	Student will...	Mark and descriptor	
A – Identification of issue and justification *(4 marks)*	... clearly identify and explain what the political issue is.	0	The work does not reach a standard described by the descriptors below.
	... explain how the issue links to the key concepts and prescribed content and of the IB Global Politics course.	1-2	The political issue raised by the engagement is implied but not explicitly identified. There is some limited explanation of why the student chose this engagement. There is some link between the engagement and course content.
		3-4	The political issue explored through the engagement is clearly and explicitly identified. There is a clear explanation of why this engagement and political issue are of interest to the student. There is a clear link between the engagement and political issue on one hand and course content on the other hand.
B – Explanation of the engagement *(4 marks)*	... clearly identify and explain what the activity was.	0	The work does not reach a standard described by the descriptors below.
	... explain the reasons why the activity was chosen, including why it was suitable for exploring and analysing the political issue that was chosen.	1-2	There is a description of the engagement and of what the student actually did. There is some limited explanation of what the student learned about global politics from undertaking the engagement.
	... explain the ways in which the activity has helped the student understand key concepts and learning outcomes that relate to the political issue chosen.	3-4	The description of the engagement and of what the student actually did is clear and relevant for their chosen political issue. There is a clear explanation of the ways in which the student's experiences informed his or her understanding of the political issue.

Criterion	Student will...	Mark and descriptor
C – Analysis of issue *(6 marks)*	... analyse the political issues raised in a wider context, particularly in light of the key concepts, learning outcomes and theoretical perspectives from each of the units in the Global Politics course. ... demonstrate evidence of research skills, organization and referencing.	0 The work does not reach a standard described by the descriptors below. 1-2 There is some attempt at analysis of the political issue but the response is largely descriptive. Few of the main points are justified. 3-4 There is some critical analysis of the political issue but this analysis lacks depth. The response is more descriptive than analytical. Some of the main points are justified. 5-6 The political issue is explored in depth, using the key concepts of the course where relevant, and the response contains clear critical analysis. All, or nearly all, of the main points are justified.
D – Synthesis and evaluation *(6 marks)*	... link together their activity and the political issue throughout the report. ... give equal attention to the activity and the report (which will read neither like an IB Extended Essay, nor like a narrative description of an activity in isolation). ... make connections with theoretical viewpoints, related ways of knowing and areas of knowledge, and multiple perspectives, giving a comprehensive treatment of the political issue that was studied.	0 The work does not reach a standard described by the descriptors below. 1-2 There are limited links between ideas. There are no conclusions, or the conclusions are not relevant. 3-4 There are some links between the student's experiences and more theoretical perspectives on the political issue. Conclusions are stated but are not entirely consistent with the evidence presented. Multiple perspectives are acknowledged, where relevant. 5-6 The student's experiences and more theoretical perspectives are synthesised so that an integrated and rich treatment of the political issue ensues. Conclusions are clearly stated, balanced and consistent with the evidence presented. There is evidence of evaluation of the political issue from multiple perspectives.

Structuring your report

Linking the issue with the key concepts (Criterion A)

One way of ensuring that students include the necessary level of analysis in their written work is to review the key concepts for each unit. For example, the 16 key concepts for the course are power, sovereignty, legitimacy, interdependence, human rights, justice, liberty, equality, development, globalization, inequality, sustainability, peace, conflict, violence, and non-violence (see pages vi and vii). Written work should explore those concepts that are relevant to the activity and political issue.

Students should make sure that they:

- define the concepts that they use
- provide examples of these concepts from world politics
- demonstrate how these concepts can be found in the activity that they engaged in.

> **Example 3: identifying the most relevant concepts**
> A student chooses to work for a local political party to encourage citizens to vote prior to an election, and they are interested in exploring how candidates for office construct and maintain their legitimacy amongst their constituents. Defining the concept of legitimacy, (perhaps as *the degree to which a political actor is accepted amongst a group of people or other political actors*) would be an important component of the engagement activity. Students could go further by identifying examples of legitimate outcomes of elections as well as those outcomes that have been deemed illegitimate by those who participated in elections or by third-party observers. A more sophisticated understanding of the concept of legitimacy would go even further; identifying the degree to which a candidate's legitimacy can depend on different constituencies at different levels of analysis in world politics.

Synonyms

sophisticated .. advanced, developed

Linking the issue and activity with prescribed content (Criteria A and B)

The chosen activity and political issue should also link with some part of the prescribed content of the course. For example, the prescribed content for the 'Power, sovereignty, and international relations' unit of the course includes the following (see pages 1–29):

- definitions and theories of power
- types of power
- the evolving nature of state sovereignty
- legitimacy of state power
- the United Nations (UN)
- intergovernmental organizations (IGOs)
- non-governmental organizations (NGOs)
- multinational corporations (MNCs)
- resistance movements
- violent protest movements
- political parties
- informal forums
- legitimacy of non-state actors
- global governance
- forms of cooperation
- forms of conflict

It would be impossible for the student to include all of these concepts in the engagement activity. However, in relation to the example of the engagement activity that focused on work for a local party, the following content could be included in the written report: types of power, political parties, legitimacy of non-state actors. Again, the student should define these terms and provide examples that demonstrate their ability to make connections between abstract terminology, examples from outside the classroom, and the activity engaged in for this study.

Justification of the issue (Criterion A)

A key assessment criterion is the degree to which the student can explain why they participated in this activity in the first place. The key here is to explain why the activity helped them explore the political issue that they chose. There is no need for students to explain how the activity helped them build other skills such as teamwork or leadership skills – this is not rewarded in the markscheme and is best avoided.

Explanation of the engagement (Criterion B)

Criterion B assesses students' ability to provide a clear account of their activity and its connection to their studies in Global Politics. This is probably the most descriptive section of the engagement activity in that students are being asked to describe all aspects of their activity as it relates to their studies of the prescribed content of the course.

Example 3: explaining your activity

Returning to **Example 3** from the previous section, the student could explain the reasons why they chose to work for a local political party and explain their efforts to get voters to the polls. The student might focus on why they feel it is important to encourage citizens to vote. Regardless of what reasons they have for pursuing a particular activity, the justification for this choice of activity is entirely up to the student and their interests.

On the one hand, the engagement activity asks students to articulate and justify their reason for political action. This can be a difficult task if students do not have a political activity that they are at least somewhat passionate about. On the other hand, this section of the engagement activity gives students the opportunity to express their interest in political issues that matter most to them. This means that they want to identify a political issue that has some value and meaning for them, and to describe their participation in such a way that it connects their understanding of the course material to the activity.

The application of students' knowledge about politics to their activity is the second section of Criterion B. Reflecting on what the student learned through the engagement activity is a critical aspect of their coursework in Global Politics and is one of the key attributes of successful IB students. As with all aspects of experiential learning activities, students should take time to debrief throughout, especially after completing their activity. Keeping a journal, or (if participating in class or group activities) taking notes during debriefing exercises, will allow students to capture their thinking about political issues as they relate to the chosen activity. Using these reflections to produce an analytical account of the student's work that demonstrates an application of their knowledge of politics, is a crucial element of the engagement activity.

Subject vocabulary

polls an election or a vote that an electorate takes part in

Synonyms

somewhat ..... a bit

General vocabulary

debrief draw conclusions from and summarize the learning as the project develops

Analysis of issue (Criterion C)

Criterion C asks students to analyse the political issue that they chose, drawing on everything that they have learned in their Global Politics coursework.

Key concepts

This criterion assesses the ability to examine political issues from a variety of perspectives. One way to think about this aspect of the engagement activity is from the frame of the key concepts in the course. The 16 key concepts, but especially those of power, sovereignty, legitimacy, and interdependence are essential to include in the analysis. For example, the student's work for a political party could lead them to be curious about the degree to which parties, candidates, or other political actors seek and reinforce their legitimacy with their constituents. Linking their conceptual understanding of legitimacy, especially with comparative examples in democratic societies and contrasting examples in non-democratic societies, will allow students to show the degree to which they can make connections between the theoretical and practical elements of their Global Politics coursework.

Extent of analysis

A second aspect of this portion of the engagement activity that students should think about is the extent to which they are analysing the political issue they chose to explore. The command term *to what extent* is an important one to understand as it is an essential part of the way that learning is assessed in the Global Politics course. Essentially, *to what extent* means that students should consider the quality of a concept or a line of reasoning in a clear and well-supported manner.

Example 3: extent of analysis
In Example 3, the experience of the engagement activity could lead a student to explore the ways in which candidates running for office use both hard power and soft power to exercise influence in an election. In this, the student might want to examine the different ways in which money is used to buy advertising, campaign resources such as consultants and activities, and other means of influencing political decision-making amongst the electorate. The analysis of the candidate's behaviour should lead the student to make a judgement as to how effective these practices were. The same method could then be applied to the ways in which the candidate led by example, attracted others to their cause, or other aspects of soft power as a way of affecting voters' decisions at the polls. In this case, the student would be making explicit connections between their experience, their conceptual understanding of different forms of power, and examining the degree to which each form of power was effective in the engagement activity.

Supporting claims

A third aspect of Criterion C is how students support the claims that they make in their analysis. Students are being assessed on how they can use evidence to support their claims. This includes:

- demonstrating a logical and organized reasoning for ideas
- using examples from their experience and the cases or material studied in the Global Politics coursework
- using examples investigated as a part of the student's research that are relevant to the topic covered in the engagement activity.

Again, in Example 3, a student would want to show that they have researched different ways in which candidates for office use different forms of power to enhance their legitimacy amongst voters. Case examples from elections or other events in the world outside the classroom can provide considerable weight in

Subject vocabulary

electorate all the people in a country who have the right to vote

support of the arguments that the student makes about the political issue they are investigating.

Synthesis and evaluation (Criterion D)

As is the case with the previous section, Criterion D asks students to align their experience in the engagement activity with the topic that they are investigating, drawing on their research and existing knowledge of global politics. Whereas Criterion C focuses on the different ways the student analyses the political issue they studied with reference to evidence, Criterion D requires them to make connections between all of their learning experiences inside and outside of the classroom along with research on the political issue they are studying. This section should also include an explicit evaluation of the student's experiences and the political issue by referring to different theoretical perspectives in order to generate a new and sophisticated understanding of politics.

There are several aspects of students' research that should be included so that they can properly synthesize and evaluate the political issue that they are studying. For example, conducting a literature review of scholarship on legitimacy and elections, or the ways in which candidates use power to secure votes, would add a level of sophistication to the argument. Balancing different views amongst a few different theoretical perspectives will allow the student to make grounded arguments about politics that highlight the complexity and nuances of the issue that they are studying. In addition, including relevant case examples as reported in leading news sources, periodicals and policy-oriented journals, supports the student's arguments in evaluating both their experience and their research.

In other words, Criterion D should reflect a diverse set of evidence that both supports students' thinking but also provides counterclaims to the arguments that they are making. Finally, the student's own interpretation of events in their experience in the engagement activity should inform the arguments and claims that they make in report. The conclusions that they arrive at, as a result of their research and experience should be clear, balanced, and most of all, align with the evidence that they have included in the report.

Summary

The engagement activity is one of the more innovative and distinct forms of assessments in the International Baccalaureate Diploma. This work will allow students to engage in an activity that connects to a political issue that interests them. In addition, students have the opportunity to integrate their classroom knowledge with what they have learned through experiences outside of a traditional lecture or classroom setting. Building on this knowledge, students have the opportunity to further investigate a political issue of interest through research and analysis at various levels. The engagement activity offers students a way of linking their understanding of the complexities of world politics with a real-life activity. Finally, the engagement activity provides a way to develop and hone students' skills in sourcing and referencing as well as excellent practice in undertaking analytical writing that is consistent within the genre of social sciences.

General vocabulary

scholarship the work of academic experts

nuances small differences in expression

counterclaims opposing arguments put forward to show that there is another point of view or analysis

innovative using new ideas or methods

hone refine or improve

Paper 1 (stimulus-based paper) technique

Paper 1 basics

Both Higher Level and Standard Level students sit the same paper which lasts 1 hour 15 minutes. This paper is a stimulus-based paper on a topic taken from one of the four core units. Four stimuli are presented, which may be written, pictorial or diagrammatic, and which link to one of the four core units. Students must answer **all** four structured questions.

The maximum mark for this paper is 25. The paper is marked using a paper-specific analytic markscheme and for the fourth question, markbands are additionally used (see below).

Each question tests different assessment objectives. **READ THE QUESTIONS FIRST** – then you can read the sources knowing what you are looking for.

Question format and advice	Assessment objective	Relevant command terms (see page x)
1. **Tests understanding of a source** You will be asked to extract information given to you in a source, which might be text, an image, or in the form of statistics. You must put it into your own words, showing that you have understood it. Five lines or so is probably about right. If you are asked to explain information from a source, take care not to simply copy the information word for word. **Top tip** Aim to get through this question quickly – take no more than 5 minutes.	Assessment objective 1: Knowledge and understanding • Demonstrate knowledge and understanding of key political concepts and contemporary issues in global politics. • Demonstrate understanding of relevant source material. • Demonstrate understanding of a political issue in a particular experiential situation (engagement activity).	**Describe** Give a detailed account. **Define** Give the precise meaning of a word, phrase, concept or physical quantity. **Identify** Provide an answer from a number of possibilities. **Outline** Give a brief account or summary.

Synonyms

contemporary present

General vocabulary

unspecified not identified or highlighted explicitly

hypothesis theory or proposition of how something works

contested where there is lack of agreement on what a concept or idea means

multi-faceted with lots of different aspects

Question format and advice	Assessment objective	Relevant command terms (see page x)
2. **Tests application of contextual knowledge to a source** You will be asked to explain a concept, using information in unspecified sources and your own knowledge. Full marks are only available if you provide examples either of your own or from the sources. **Top tips** The questions may be linked to the key concepts of the syllabus. Revise the definitions of these. Don't forget to use the sources to help you, too – you are asked to do this. Refer to more than one source if possible. Some concepts that you are asked to analyse may be contested or multi-faceted. If so, bring this out in your analysis, demonstrating your own knowledge. For example, a question analysing power may require you to show that power is a broader concept than the material in the sources suggests. Aim to spend 10 minutes or so on this question and write about 200-250 words.	Assessment objective 2: Application and analysis ● Apply knowledge of key political concepts to analyse contemporary political issues in a variety of contexts. ● Identify and analyse relevant material and supporting examples. ● Use political concepts and examples to formulate, present and sustain an argument. ● Apply knowledge of global politics to inform and analyse experiential learning about a political issue (engagement activity).	**Analyse** Break down in order to bring out the essential elements or structure. **Distinguish** Make clear the differences between two or more concepts or items. **Explain** Give a detailed account including reasons or causes. **Suggest** Propose a solution, hypothesis or other possible answer.

Question format and advice	Assessment objective	Relevant command terms (see page x)
3. **Tests comparison and / or contrasting of sources** You will be asked to compare and contrast the views in two different or contradictory sources. **Top tips** Aim for at least four points of comparison, contrast or both (depending on the command term used). Clearly devote equal consideration to both sources. There is no need for your own views on which source is more credible / convincing. Highlight what the source is – is one a news article and the other an NGO report, for example? What relevance does the type of source have? Aim to spend around 25 minutes on this question and write at least 300 words.	Assessment objective 3: Synthesis and evaluation ● Compare, contrast, synthesize and evaluate evidence from sources and background knowledge. ● Compare, contrast, synthesize and evaluate a variety of perspectives and approaches to global politics, and evaluate political beliefs, biases and prejudices, and their origin. ● Synthesize and evaluate results of experiential learning and more theoretical perspectives on a political issue (engagement activity). Assessment objective 4: Use and application of appropriate skills ● Produce well-structured written material that uses appropriate terminology. ● Organize material into a clear, logical, coherent and relevant response. ● Demonstrate evidence of research skills, organization and referencing (engagement activity and HL extension in particular).	**Compare and contrast** Give an account of similarities and differences between two (or more) items or situations, referring to both (all) of them throughout. **Contrast** Give an account of the differences between two (or more) items or situations, referring to both (all) of them throughout. **Compare** Give an account of the similarities between two (or more) items or situations, referring to both (all) of them throughout.

Question format and advice	Assessment objective	Relevant command terms (see page x)
4. **Tests evaluation of sources and contextual knowledge** **AO3:** Compare and contrast, and evaluate source material. Synthesize and evaluate evidence from both sources and your own knowledge. **AO4:** Organize material into a clear, logical, and coherent response. The question will be a Paper 2 style question, demanding a longer response based on the issues raised by the sources. Think of this question as a paper 2 style question but one where you have some sources to help you. **Top tips** Use the sources to help you: don't ignore them and don't only use your own knowledge. You are being tested on your ability to use sources as well as your own knowledge. Use examples – from the sources and your own knowledge. Include claim and counterclaim, balance and clear evaluation etc. Keep your focus on the question, refer back to the question frequently to build your argument as you go along. Define any key terms. Aim for a short introduction and conclusion. Aim to spend around 30 minutes on this question and write at least 600 words.	Assessment objective 3: Synthesis and evaluation ● Compare, contrast, synthesize and evaluate evidence from sources and background knowledge. ● Compare, contrast, synthesize and evaluate a variety of perspectives and approaches to global politics, and evaluate political beliefs, biases and prejudices, and their origin. ● Synthesize and evaluate results of experiential learning and more theoretical perspectives on a political issue (engagement activity). Assessment objective 4: Use and application of appropriate skills ● Produce well-structured written material that uses appropriate terminology. ● Organize material into a clear, logical, coherent and relevant response. ● Demonstrate evidence of research skills, organization and referencing (engagement activity and HL extension in particular).	**Discuss** Offer a considered and balanced review that includes a range of arguments, factors or hypotheses. Opinions or conclusions should be presented clearly and supported by appropriate evidence. **Evaluate** Make an appraisal by weighing up the strengths and limitations. **Examine** Consider an argument or concept in a way that uncovers the assumptions and interrelationships of the issue.

Markbands for the fourth question

Marks	Level descriptor
0	● The work does not reach a standard described by the descriptors below.
1–2	● There is a very limited understanding of the demands of the question. ● There is little relevant knowledge. ● The response is mostly descriptive and may contain unsupported generalizations.
3–4	● There is a limited understanding of the demands of the question, or the question is only partially addressed. ● Some knowledge is demonstrated, but this is not always relevant or accurate, and may not be used appropriately or effectively. ● Counterclaims, or different views on the question, are not identified.
5–6	● The response shows an understanding of the demands of the question. ● Knowledge is mostly accurate and relevant, and there is some limited synthesis of own knowledge and source material. ● Counterclaims, or different views on the question, are implicitly identified but are not explored.
7–8	● The response is focused and shows a good understanding of the demands of the question. ● Relevant and accurate knowledge is demonstrated, there is a synthesis of own knowledge and source material, and appropriate examples are used. ● Counterclaims, or different views on the question, are explored.
9–10	● The response is clearly focused and shows a high degree of understanding of the demands of the question. ● Relevant and accurate knowledge is demonstrated, there is effective synthesis of own knowledge and source material, with appropriate examples integrated. ● Counterclaims, or different views on the question, are explored and evaluated.

The following is an example of a claim and counterclaim being identified, explored and evaluated.

Question: *Evaluate the claim that the importance of military power is diminishing in modern global politics.*

Possible claim: Military power still relevant, as seen in the conflicts in Afghanistan and Iraq in 2001 and 2003 respectively. Powerful states, such as the United States, chose to use military power to achieve their objectives.

Possible counterclaim: However, despite this use of military power, its effectiveness and therefore its importance is questionable. In both of these conflicts mentioned (Iraq and Afghanistan) military power led to inconclusive outcomes.

Paper 2 (extended response paper) technique

Paper 2 Basics

Each Paper 2 question is marked out of 25.

Higher Level students must answer three questions in 2 hours and 45 minutes. Standard Level students must answer two questions in 1 hour 45 minutes.

This paper is an essay paper, with two questions set on each of the four core units. At least one of the questions for each unit is firmly anchored in that unit, whereas the second question may open up for a more cross-unit approach.

Conceptual understanding and ability to work with the key concepts of the course is particularly important in this paper. Some questions use the key concepts of that particular unit. Still other questions draw on key concepts from several units. Even where the key concepts are not explicitly mentioned in a question, students should demonstrate a conceptual understanding of global politics. In their answers, students are invited to draw on their understanding of any relevant political concepts, depending on the arguments they put forward.

Marks are awarded for:

- demonstrating understanding of relevant political concepts and prescribed content
- making reference to specific relevant examples
- justifying points
- and exploring and evaluating counterclaims, or different views on the question.

The same paper is set at both SL and HL.

SL students must answer **two** questions, each selected from a **different** core unit.

HL students must answer **three** questions, each selected from a **different** core unit.

The maximum mark for this paper is 50 marks at SL and 75 marks at HL. The paper is marked using generic markbands (see pages 125-126) and a paper-specific markscheme. The questions in this paper assess objectives AO1-AO4, and questions are set using AO3 command terms (see page x).

Paper 2 overview

Core unit	Key concepts	Learning outcomes	Possible questions
Power, sovereignty and international relations	Power Sovereignty Legitimacy Interdependence	● Nature of power ● Operation of state power in global politics ● Function and impact of international organizations and non-state actors in global politics ● Nature and extent of interactions in global politics	Evaluate the claim that the importance of military power is diminishing in modern global politics. Evaluate the claim that the only legitimate actors in global politics are nation states. Discuss how globalization has affected both the interdependence of states and the balance of power in the international system. 'Global politics is characterized more by conflict than by cooperation'. Discuss. *Questions that link between this unit and other units:* 'Nation states are the biggest obstacle to global human rights protection'. Discuss. Compare and contrast a state-led approach to resolving violent conflict with an approach led by other international actors.
Human rights	Human rights Justice Liberty Equality	● Nature and evolution of human rights ● Codification, protection and monitoring of human rights ● Practice of human rights ● Debates surrounding human rights and their application: differing interpretations of justice, liberty and equality	'A national or regional approach to human rights enforcement is more effective than a global approach'. Discuss. Evaluate the extent to which universal human rights challenge state sovereignty. To what extent do the complex realities and relationships of power in global politics make the concept of human rights an unachievable ideal? Examine the claim that different interpretations of human rights by states, cultures and people are unjustifiable in modern global politics. Has globalization made the protection of human rights more or less difficult? Discuss. *Questions that link between this unit and other units:* Evaluate the extent to which universal human rights challenge state sovereignty. Evaluate the extent to which a lack of human rights impacts on development. Evaluate the importance of justice and human rights in resolving violent and non-violent conflict.

Core unit	Key concepts	Learning outcomes	Possible questions
Development	Development Globalization Inequality Sustainability	● Contested meanings of development ● Factors that may promote or inhibit development ● Pathways towards development ● Debates surrounding development: challenges of globalization, inequality and sustainability	Evaluate the claim that there is a link between globalization and poverty. 'Development failures stem from factors that are internal to states, rather than external'. Discuss. Evaluate the claim that development is impossible to measure. To what extent are most pathways to development based on purely Western approaches to development? *Questions that link between this unit and other units:* 'There is no security without development, and no development without security'. To what extent do you agree? 'Conflict powerfully inhibits development, and equally, failures in development substantially increase the likelihood of conflict' (Paul Collier, *The Bottom Billion*). To what extent do you agree with this claim?
Peace and conflict	Peace Conflict Violence Non-violence	● Contested meanings of peace, conflict and violence ● Causes and **parties to** conflict ● Evolution of conflict ● Conflict resolution and post-conflict transformation	'Transforming violent conflict towards peace relies on an interrelationship of peacemaking, peacekeeping and peacebuilding'. Discuss. To what extent is modern conflict caused by competition for power? To what extent is third party involvement in conflict (for example, through humanitarian or other intervention) beneficial for advancing peace and reducing conflict? To what extent do you agree with the view that those in power have an obligation to identify and prevent structural violence? *Questions that link between this unit and other units:* Evaluate the claim that violations of human rights are no guarantee that humanitarian intervention will take place. 'A key part of achieving positive peace is the availability of a system of justice to settle differences non-violently'. To what extent do you agree?

Paper 2 Top tips

- Define the key terms of the question in your introduction. For example, if the question asks you to 'discuss how <u>globalization</u> has affected the <u>interdependence of states</u> and the <u>balance of power</u> in the international system', you must define the key terms underlined here.

- Explain briefly in your introduction how you intend to answer the question.

- Use plenty of contemporary examples to back up your arguments, ideally ones from within your lifetime.

- Root your arguments in the relevant theories and concepts that you have studied. This might be hard or soft power, sovereignty etc.

- Build your argument as you go and refer back to the question. This is what marks out really high standard politics essays. Only make a point if it helps you to answer the question. When you have made a point, state how this helps answer the question. Use phrases like 'this shows that...' when summing up a point you have just made.

- Avoid using the first person – there is no need for 'I believe that...' or 'in my opinion...'.

- Aim for balance. Always look at the other side of the argument. High marks are available for students who use claims and counterclaims in their answers. Put forward one side of the argument and then contrast it immediately with other views and state which – on the balance of the evidence – is more powerful.

- Better to focus on fundamental points well explained, than ambitious guesses or new theories that are poorly explained. Only explore more radical thoughts once you have been through the fundamental arguments.

- Take time to explain your points. Do not rush or try to make a complicated point in one sentence. Use the first few sentences to set out your argument carefully.

- Responses should deal with the whole question not just the separate parts.

- Do not rush your conclusion. See it as a fundamental part of your essay rather than something to tick off. Check that your conclusion answers the question. Take your time to summarize the most important points and pieces of evidence which have led you to that conclusion.

Structuring a response

Introduction	<ul><li>Define the key terms.</li><li>Explain how you will answer the question.</li></ul>
Main paragraphs	<ul><li>Subsequent paragraphs should develop one point only each.</li><li>Follow this structure for paragraphs:<ul><li>**Point** – make the main statement of the paragraph.</li><li>**Evidence** or **Example** – this is the longest part of your paragraph.</li><li>**Analyse** – why does the evidence back up your point?</li><li>**Link** – relate the paragraph to the main question with a one sentence mini conclusion or counterclaim.</li></ul></li></ul>
Conclusion	<ul><li>Summarize points already made – explain what the balance of evidence leads you to conclude and which side is most persuasive.</li><li>Answer the question.</li></ul>

Example paragraph structure

'Nation states should be forced to accept universal human rights'. Discuss.

POINT — Prisoner voting rights is a controversial issue within Western countries where the universality of those rights is questioned. The United Kingdom currently has a **blanket ban** on prisoners voting in any form of UK election.

EVIDENCE/ EXAMPLE — In a **landmark** case, Hirst v UK, the European Court of Human Rights (ECHR) ruled that the blanket ban on prisoners exercising the vote was contrary to the ECHR to which the UK is a **signatory**. The UK appealed, stating that it was the sovereign right of its parliament to represent the majority wish of the British people to maintain the ban, but the decision was upheld by the ECHR. This demonstrates that, in countries with well-developed national human rights laws and democratic processes such as the UK, there are still differences of opinion with universal human rights as interpreted by regional and international bodies.

ANALYSE — In the UK, the concept of parliamentary sovereignty means that the UK's democratically elected MPs in parliament have the power to make or unmake any law, so long as it is compatible with the UK's Human Rights Act. In summary, this raises the question of whether democratic decisions taken by elected bodies should be overruled by international bodies promoting universal rights but with no direct democratic right to do so.

LINK — Universalists would argue that universal rights are, by definition, beyond the scope of democratic debate.

Model essay plans

Discuss how globalization has affected both the interdependence of states and the balance of power in the international system.

The essay will include a definition of 'globalization' as *the increasing global interconnectedness of political, economic and cultural life*. In a globalized world, our lives are increasingly shaped by events that occur, and decisions that are made, at a distance from us. The concept, which is a contested one for sceptics and a reality for **hyperglobalists**, argues that geographical distance is of declining importance and that territorial borders are becoming less significant.

'Balance of power' refers to a condition in which no one state predominates over others, tending to create general equilibrium and limit the **hegemonic** ambition of all states. 'Interdependence' refers to the notion that all states have common interests, where each is affected by decisions taken by the other.

General vocabulary

blanket ban complete prohibition of something

landmark significant development

signatory referring to a state that has signed a piece of international law

hegemonic relating to a state or an actor in global politics that is more powerful than all others

Subject vocabulary

hyperglobalists those who believe that globalization has radically changed modern global political structures and systems

Claim: Globalization has affected interdependence / balance of power	Counterclaim: Globalization has not affected interdependence / balance of power
Liberal view • Globalization has brought new era where nation state less important as a lone actor, international cooperation and interdependence the new reality. • With the nation state no longer the dominant actor, a more stable, equitable balance of power is possible.	**Realist view** • Globalization overstated. Sceptics vs hyperglobalists. • Nation states still remain important. Economic interdependence is intensifying rather than an interlocking global economy. 'More of the same' rather than a radical change.
Political globalization to solve common problems • Climate change, organized crime, pandemic disease. • Globalization (including removal of borders, freer movement of people, goods and information) means shared problems require global political institutions to solve them (EU, UN, AU). • Pooling of sovereignty.	**Anarchy more the model than interdependence** • States remain self-interested and increased economic interdependence is more likely to lead to conflict than cooperation.
Balance of power • Concept of a global hegemon in decline. Rise of the BRIC (Brazil, Russia, India, China) countries with GDP faster than traditional Western powers. • Globalized economic market is responsible for this. • Frameworks of global governance (UN UDHR, IMF, WTO, UN) are reducing the power of nation-states and establishing a more stable balance of power between nation states where one is less able to dominate.	**Globalization created by states** • Made by states, for states, particularly dominant states. • Organizations such as the UN still maintain a certain balance of power, e.g. the UN Security Council dominated by five 'world powers' with veto power.
Economic globalization • National economies absorbed into one globalized economy.	**Globalization is a cause of conflict and instability** • Terrorist groups, for example, are creating an imbalance of power and have led to a decade of disorder post-9/11 with many wars where asymmetric warfare has challenged the great powers.

Subject vocabulary

asymmetric warfare conflict in which there is an imbalance between the parties, for example, in aims, capacity or strategy

To what extent is sovereignty an outdated concept in the 21st century?

Answers will include an explanation of the concept of sovereignty as the principle of absolute and unlimited power over a defined territory and population, including the notion of internal and external sovereignty (power within a state versus power on the world stage). Reference may be made to sovereignty as originating from the Peace of Westphalia in 1648.

Claim: Sovereignty is an outdated concept	Counterclaim: Sovereignty is not an outdated concept
Liberal view • Globalization has been marked by the decline of the nation state: power shifting away from the state to non-state actors, global interdependence more important, the 'internationalization of the state' (Cox, 1993).	**Realist view** • Nation state still the basic unit of the international system.
Permeable borders • State borders, once the guarantee of territorial state sovereignty, are permeable. • International tourism, movement of knowledge and information via the internet. • Global financial markets and transnational capital flows – economic sovereignty redundant.	**Borderless world a myth** • National economies still exist and much economic activity takes place within state borders as well as outside. • States choose to engage in global economy.
Rise of non-state actors • TNCs wield greater power than many nation states, can dictate state policy by relocating elsewhere. NGOs. Terrorist groups. Whistle-blowers. IGOs (EU, UN, UN Security Council).	**States remain dominant** • Exercise power in a way that no other global actor can. • Control over what happens in territory is rarely challenged. Only failed states have lost control over what happens within their borders.
International human rights • Notion of responsible sovereignty, R2P and humanitarian intervention. • International norm developed whereby nation states surrender their sovereignty if they mistreat their population. • Standards of conduct (UN UDHR) to which all states must conform.	**Pooled sovereignty** • IGOs are created by states, for states. • Pooling sovereignty means greater influence and capacity than if acting alone.
Collective dilemmas • Climate change, organized crime, terrorism, international migration, pandemic diseases.	**Enduring attraction of nation state** • Nation states will not lose their dominance as long as they enjoy the allegiance of the mass of their citizens. • Or allegiances based on religion, culture or ethnicity unlikely to thrive.

There may be reference to specific examples of threats to sovereignty including TNCs, IGOs, terrorist groups; collective dilemmas such as climate change or organized crime; humanitarian intervention in the former Yugoslavia.

There may be reference to specific examples of the state's enduring importance, for example in the sphere of international action (Russia and Ukraine sovereignty dispute over Crimea in 2014).

Paper 2 markbands

Marks	Level descriptor
0	● The work does not reach a standard described by the descriptors below.
1–5	● The response reveals limited understanding of the demands of the question. ● The response is poorly structured, or where there is a recognizable essay structure there is minimal focus on the task. ● There is little relevant knowledge, and examples are either lacking or not relevant. ● The response is mostly descriptive.
6–10	● The response indicates some understanding of the demands of the question. ● There is some evidence of an attempt to structure the response. ● Some relevant knowledge is present, and some examples are mentioned but they are not developed or their relevance to arguments is not clear. ● The response demonstrates limited understanding of the key concepts of the course. ● There is limited justification of main points. ● Counterclaims, or different views on the question, are not considered.
11–15	● The demands of the question are understood and mostly addressed but the implications are not considered. ● There is a clear attempt to structure the response. ● The response is mostly based on relevant and accurate knowledge of global politics, and relevant examples are given and support arguments. ● The response demonstrates some understanding of the key concepts of the course. ● Many of the main points are justified and arguments are largely coherent. ● Some counterclaims, or different views on the question, are considered.

Marks	Level descriptor
16–20	• The demands of the questions are understood and addressed, and most implications are considered. • The response is well-structured. • The response demonstrates relevant and accurate knowledge and understanding of global politics, and relevant examples are used in a way that strengthens arguments. • The response demonstrates a good grasp of the key concepts of the course. • All or nearly all of the main points are justified and arguments are coherent. • Counterclaims, or different views on the question, are explored.
21–25	• A very well structured and balanced response that addresses the demands and implications of the question. • Comprehensive knowledge and in-depth understanding of global politics is applied in the response consistently and effectively, with examples integrated. • The response demonstrates a very good grasp of the key concepts of the course. • All of the main points are justified. Arguments are clear, coherent and compelling. • Counterclaims, or different views on the question, are explored and evaluated.

Introduction

One of the requirements of the IB Diploma is to write an Extended Essay. An Extended Essay is an in-depth study of a limited topic within a particular subject area. It provides the opportunity to carry out independent research within a subject of your choice. A good research question is essential for Extended Essay success. Many students find the Extended Essay a useful resource to draw on in interviews for university or employment.

This leads to a major piece of formally presented, structured writing, in which ideas and findings are communicated in a reasoned and coherent manner, appropriate to the subject chosen. It is mandatory that all students undertake three reflection sessions with their supervisor, which includes a short, concluding interview, or *viva voce*, with their supervisor following the completion of the Extended Essay. An assessment of this reflection process is made under Criterion E (engagement) using the 'Reflections on planning and progress' form.

Whichever subject is chosen, the Extended Essay is concerned with exploring a specific research question through interpreting and evaluating evidence, and constructing reasoned arguments. In undertaking the Extended Essay, students model many of the elements of academic research by locating their topic within a broader disciplinary context, or issue in the case of a world studies Extended Essay. They will justify the relevance of their research and critically evaluate the overall strength of the arguments made and sources used. Guided through this process by a supervisor, students are encouraged to reflect on insights gained, evaluate decisions and respond to challenges encountered during the research.

Reflection in the Extended Essay

- Reflection in the Extended Essay focuses on the student's progress during the planning, research and writing process. It is intended to help students with the development of their Extended Essay as well as allowing them the opportunity to consider the effectiveness of their choices, to re-examine their ideas and to decide whether changes are needed.
- The emphasis in the Extended Essay is on process reflection, characterized by reflecting on conceptual understandings, decision-making, engagement with data, the research process, time management, methodology, successes and challenges, and the appropriateness of sources.
- Students will be encouraged to informally reflect throughout the experience of researching and writing the Extended Essay, but are required to reflect formally during the reflection sessions with their supervisor and when completing the 'Reflections on planning and progress' form.

General guidelines for all Extended Essays

All students must:
- provide a logical and coherent rationale for their choice of topic
- review what has already been written about the topic
- formulate a clear research question
- offer a concrete description of the methods they use to investigate the question
- generate reasoned interpretations and conclusions based on their reading and independent research in order to answer the question.

Overview of the assessment criteria for the Extended Essay

Criterion A: focus and method	Criterion B: knowledge and understanding	Criterion C: critical thinking	Criterion D: presentation	Criterion E: engagement
• Topic • Research question • Methodology	• Context • Subject-specific terminology and concepts	• Research • Analysis • Discussion and evaluation	• Structure • Layout	• Process • Research focus
Marks	**Marks**	**Marks**	**Marks**	**Marks**
6	6	12	4	6

Total marks available: 34

The Extended Essay criteria and advice to achieve high marks for each criterion

Criterion and Marks	Advice/questions to ask yourself
A: focus and method – 6 marks • Topic • Research question • Methodology	**Topic:** There is no substitute for solid reading before choosing your topic and getting to know it really well. The danger is writing too soon, before you have enough knowledge. Be broad in what you read – vary the type of source (books, journals, documentary, news, blogs) and read a wide range of views from a wide range of sources (for example, if researching the Israel and Palestine question, views from many perspectives will be needed: Israel, Palestine, UN, EU, other IGOs, NGOs, etc.). You are aiming for about 20 different sources. **Research question:** Choose one that you can reasonably analyse in good depth in 4,000 words. Examples of well-focused research questions include: 'How successful has Putin been in decreasing Russia's internal security threat from the North Caucasus 1999–2009?' and 'To what extent was the US involvement in Afghanistan about US state security?' They are good because they are country specific (they avoid analysing more than one country) and time specific (the best time frame is 2–5 years but no more than 10). Make sure the answer to your question requires analysis rather than description. Get yourself a working title and begin your research. Your question may change, but be fairly sure about the scope from the beginning. **Bibliography:** It is never too early to start this. It is better to include everything as you research and write than to try to fill in the gaps at the end of the process.

B: knowledge and understanding – 6 marks	• Have you explained how your research question relates to the specific subject you selected for the Extended Essay?

B: knowledge and understanding – 6 marks

- Context
- Subject-specific terminology and concepts

• Have you explained how your research question relates to the specific subject you selected for the Extended Essay?

• Have you used relevant terminology and concepts throughout your essay as they relate to your particular area of research?

• Is it clear that the sources you are using are relevant and appropriate to your research question?

• Do you have a range of sources, or have you only relied on one particular type, for example, internet sources?

• Is there a reason why you might not have a range? Is this justified?

C: critical thinking – 12 marks

- Research
- Analysis
- Discussion and evaluation

Research sources: Sources will need to be tailored to individual essays and research questions.

• For scholarly, academic texts, a subscription to the academic journal library JSTOR is useful.

• In the news media, *The Economist*, *Foreign Affairs*, *The Financial Times*, *The New York Times*, *The Washington Post*, the BBC, Al Jazeera and other regional and national titles relevant to your topic will all be useful.

• Useful think tanks might include the Royal United Services Institute or the Council on Foreign Relations.

• Government departments can be useful sources, such as the Foreign and Commonwealth Office (UK) and the State Department (US).

• IGOs such as the European Union, the United Nations (and its sub-agencies, such as the UN Development Programme, the Security Council or the Human Rights Council), the IMF, the World Bank and many others.

• NGOs such as Oxfam, Amnesty International and Human Rights Watch.

• To get a basic understanding of your topic, if you are new to the topic, establish a basic timeline of events (websites such as the BBC can be useful). Record all sources including a consideration of the reliability of each one.

Analysis and skeleton plan: Create a skeleton plan for your essay – see the example structure below.

- Introduction
- Section / key theme 1
- Section / key theme 2
- Section / key theme 3
- Conclusion

Often, dividing the essay into this structure helps to break the essay down into manageable sections. Focusing on three key themes, all of which help to answer the research question can be a good idea. Each section can be thought of as a mini-essay that supports the overall research question. Also see the developed skeleton plan at the end of this 'Extended essay' section.

As you read each source, note down key quotations that seem important or around which you may later want to structure an argument. Put the quotations into the relevant sections of the essay. Put arguments that you think are important into the skeleton structure in your own words, in note form. You can come back to them later when drafting and tidy them up. You can also link them to other sources, statistics or evidence to back up your argument. This saves time and gives your reading a real focus.

D: presentation – 4 marks

- Structure
- Layout

- Have you chosen a font that will be easy for examiners to read on-screen?
- Is your essay double-spaced and typed up in size 12 font?
- Are the title and research question mentioned on the cover page?
- Are all pages numbered?
- Have you prepared a correct table of contents?
- Do the page numbers in the table of contents match the page numbers in the text?
- Are all figures and tables properly numbered and labelled?
- Does your bibliography contain only the sources cited in the text?
- Did you use the same reference system throughout the essay?
- Does the essay have less than 4,000 words?
- Is all the material presented in the appendices relevant and necessary?
- Have you proofread the text for spelling or grammar errors?

Stucture: It helps to divide the essay into an introduction (300 words), three chapters (approx. 1,100 words each) analysing three key areas, then a conclusion (300 words). Another option is to write five sections of 600 words each. Treat each chapter like an essay in its own right, but clearly link each one to the question and the rest of the essay. The introduction has a specific purpose – to state the research question and why it is worthy of research. This is all you should include in your introduction. Long sections of historical narrative that describe rather than analyse are rarely needed.

E: engagement – 6 marks

- Process
- Research focus

Research focus:

- Have you demonstrated your engagement with your research topic and the research process?
- Have you highlighted challenges you faced and how you overcame them?
- Will the examiner get a sense of your intellectual and skills development?
- Will the examiner get a sense of your creativity and intellectual initiative?
- Will the examiner get a sense of how you responded to actions and ideas in the research process?

Process: Only start writing once you:

- know what your answer is to the research question
- know several very strong arguments in each chapter that will support that answer
- know what other arguments are out there that challenge your position and how you will counter these
- know what other arguments / evidence support your position and how you can use these
- are sure of the key three chapters / themes / sub-topics that are most important to your question.

Skeleton plan

To what extent did Pakistan support the United States in the 'War on Terror' between 2001 and 2011?

Introduction – Explain why the research question is worthy of study. Why did it matter that Pakistan did support the US in the 'War on Terror'? Was it a legitimate demand of Pakistan from the US?

Section/key theme 1 – During 2001–2008 Pakistan was under military rule (President Musharraf). This provides a distinct period which can be analysed. It was a period marked by a publicly close relationship between President George W. Bush and President Musharraf, but what was the real extent of Pakistani support for the US?

Section/key theme 2 – From 2008 Pakistan was under civilian rule and the government changed. President Musharraf left office and was replaced by a civilian president, President Zardari. Did this change from military to civilian rule have any impact on the extent of Pakistani support? At this point, too, President Obama took office in the US. What impact did this have?

Secition/key theme 3 – A major moment in the US–Pakistani relationship during the 'War on Terror' was the discovery and assassination of Osama Bin Laden. This was one of the major goals of the US in the 'War on Terror', and yet it was achieved in spite of, rather than because of, Pakistani cooperation. What does this tell us about the support that Pakistan provided the US in the 'War on Terror'?

Conclusion – Where does the balance of evidence lie? Did Pakistan support the US in the 'War on Terror'? If not, why was this support not provided? What challenges or viewpoints prevented this?

Index

W

Improve your learning

Take a look at some of the interactive tools on your **Pearson Baccalaureate Essentials Global Politics** eText. Note that the examples below may be from a different title, but you will find topic-appropriate resources on your eText.

Vocabulary lists

Complete vocabulary lists help support you to understand any unusual terms.

Theory of Knowledge

Aboriginal people the people who have been in a region since ancient times
abstract existing in thought as an idea without an actual existence
abstract ideas existing in thought as an idea without actual existence
abstractions things reduced to their most basic characteristics
acquired to have taken possession or ownership of
adopted legally made part of a family that someone was not born into
agnostics people who doubt that there is a God
agricultural purposes related to farming
algebra the part of mathematics that uses letters and other general symbols to represent numbers, and quantities in formulae and equations
Allah the Muslim name for God
altruistic unselfish, willing to make sacrifices
ambiguity confusion because words or sentences have more than one meaning
Amish a Christian group living in old-fashioned ways in Pennsylvania and Ohio
...sing engaging in a detailed examination ...detailed examination
...netry the branch of algebra that ...ric objects such as points, lines,

atheists people who do not believe ... deities
atom the smallest component of an ... living thing
audience participation the ability of t... to take part, ask questions
authoritarian governments governme... concentrate power in the hands of o... small group; people are not given fr... rights
authority figures people in a position ... over someone else
authority right to be believed or hav...
autism a mental condition that beg... childhood and which causes diffi... human communication and lan...
awakening reaching a higher le...
axioms basic rules in mathema... considered to be absolute...

Babylon Noah's city in i... was the capital of a...
Behaviourists psy... observable,...
biases opi... ide...

1.1 Introduction to cells

PDF

Main idea
In many celled organisms, individual cells take on specific tasks. Individual cells may replace damaged or diseased cells when needed.

Understanding: According to the cell theory, living organisms are composed of cells.

Model sentence: **The cell theory states that organisms are made up of one or more cells.**

- Some living organisms are composed of only one cell, such as *Paramecium*. These organisms are referred to as unicellular.
- Multicellular organisms, such as trees and birds, are composed of many cells.

Hints for success: Whenever the term organism is used, think of cells and life.

Nature of science: **In biology, there are often exceptions to theories and belief There are exceptions to the cell theory statement that says all organisms are made up of cells.**

...ntists recognize that exceptions to the cell theory include giant fun... ...not have walls separating cells, and striated muscle cells i...

...ulary
...tant cellular
...that all
...of one or
...e smallest
...ome from
...v exist
...ng the

Audio

Audio versions of definitions and articulation sentences help you to understand and unlock key information.

Interactive glossary

A searchable audio glossary gives you a handy reference tool for any difficult words, with audio to support your learning. Select highlighted words in the text to hear the audio version of the term and definition.

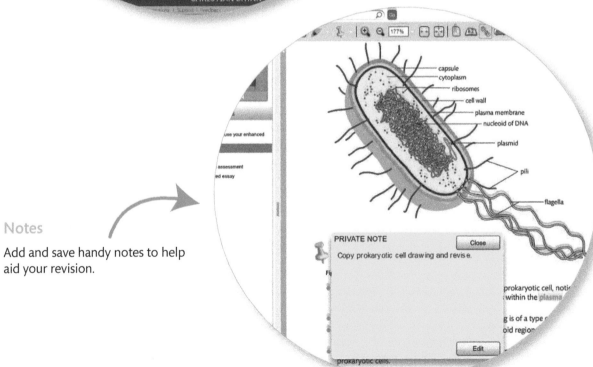

Notes

Add and save handy notes to help aid your revision.